Explaining and questioning

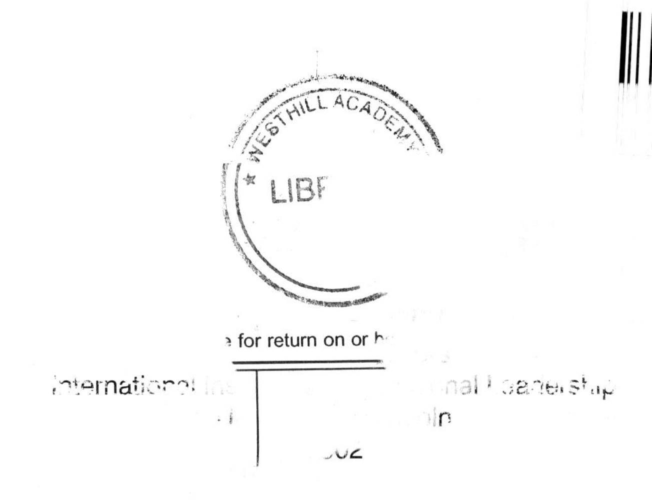

Text © Trevor Kerry 2002

The right of Trevor Kerry to be identified as author of this work has been asserted by him in accordance with the Copyright, Designs and Patents Act 1988.

All rights reserved. No part of this publication may be reproduced or transmitted in any form or by any means, electronic or mechanical, including photocopy, recording or any information storage and retrieval system, without permission in writing from the publisher or under licence from the Copyright Licensing Agency Limited, of 90 Tottenham Court Road, London W1T 4LP.

Any person who commits any unauthorised act in relation to this publication may be liable to criminal prosecution and civil claims for damages.

Published in 2002 by:
Nelson Thornes Ltd
Delta Place
27 Bath Road
CHELTENHAM
GL53 7TH
United Kingdom

06 / 10 9 8 7 6 5 4 3

A catalogue record for this book is available from the British Library

ISBN 0 7487 6859 9

Page make-up by Acorn Bookwork, Salisbury

Printed and bound in Croatia by Zrinski

Contents

Foreword

The material in this book was published previously as *Questioning and Explaining*, and this volume has been subject to a number of significant revisions and updates. The book is prefaced by a new editorial and a revised section on how to use the manual. All the material has been linked specifically with the National Standards for teacher education, and there are connections made to other government reports and papers. New material on research and on the roles of support staff has been included. While the text and Activities remain mainly unchanged, each chapter is preceded and concluded with a panel to guide the reader's learning. Dated material has been excised. The intention is that, in its new format, the material – all of which has been composed and trialled in real classrooms and with teachers undergoing professional development – will help Key Stage 2 and 3 teachers along with students in training for these age-groups to gain immediate access to these crucial skills.

EDITORIAL

The world of education, and above all of educational organisations, changes at an ever-increasing pace, but the need for teaching skills remains a constant in this sea of change. Of course, the skills themselves have to be reassessed, updated, amended and refined. This is the purpose of the present series of books: to take a practical but analytical look at teaching pupils at Key Stages 2 and 3.

The series brings together experts in the field of pedagogy, covering key issues in the art and science of teaching. It is interesting to reflect that, after 150 years of compulsory education for all children, this country still does not have any posts in colleges or universities that are overtly about teaching skills, i.e. pedagogy. There are lecturers in subject areas, professors in education, and education management gurus – but not a single professor of pedagogy. That fact alone must indicate the value that books like this have in helping practitioners in a far too neglected field.

The series is deliberately cross-phase in its approach. There are two reasons for this. The first is that the fundamental skills required of the teacher at these two levels are essentially the same or similar. The second reason is that the latest government thinking, encapsulated in its 2001 White Paper, highlights both the transition from primary to secondary schools and what it sees as the relatively poor performance of Key Stage 3 teachers. Indeed, the Government implies that it would like to see approaches at Key Stage 3 become more like those at Key Stage 2. However, while governments define policy, it is left to practitioners to work out those policies in practice, as here.

But this series also has a context in those very educational changes that we have mentioned. The teaching profession, at every level, is still coming to terms with two decades of far-reaching innovation. These are just a few of the, universally significant, events that have happened in that time:

- The establishment of governing bodies with extensive powers and legal responsibilities
- The introduction of a National Curriculum along with several major emendations of it and its operation
- The requirement for teachers to undertake professional training and development on a minimum number of days per year
- The reform of educational finances and the growth of cheque-book schools
- The demise of Local Educational Authority powers in many areas of operation
- The institution of Ofsted inspections
- Requirements for appraisal of teachers
- The compulsion for assessment of pupils through SATs
- The insistence of the Government that schools publish their league tables of results

- The introduction of literacy and numeracy hours in primary schools – a move towards increased prescription over what is taught, and how it is taught
- Compulsory processes for the monitoring of the performance of head teachers
- The positive and financially tangible encouragement of the adoption of ICT as a fundamental way of working in schools
- Innovative routes into teaching such as the SCITT schemes
- The rise in the use, and variety of use, of support staff in schools
- Encouragement of the establishment of schemes of private–public partnership in school funding
- New standards published by the Teacher Training Agency for the training of teachers.

The list could be extended, but the reader will already have grasped the enormity of change on the professional life of teachers. The list doesn't deal with the more intangible changes that permeate the education environment: changes to philosophy, theory and approach. These include things as varied, and as wide-ranging, as: the growth of concern in educational psychology with multiple intelligences; the imposition of political philosophies such as marketing schools; the invention of management practices such as reengineering; the growth of practical proposals such as changing the school calendar from three to five or six terms; or conditions of service issues such as the introduction of performance-related pay. What an exciting and varied life we in the teaching profession lead!

In this ocean of innovation, teaching skills remain an island of calm on which all who provide services to pupils in classrooms must retain their hold and on which they must focus. Teaching skills are not a refuge from change: indeed they change with the shifting situation. But they are root skills that teachers need. In this series we look at some of those key skills, reinterpreting them for today's classrooms and learning situations, and recognising the continuing and important role they play in realising the potential of students and pupils. The series covers such essential topics as managing the classroom efficiently, formulating learning objectives, asking effective questions, explaining clearly, setting worthwhile tasks to pupils, and using ICT to best advantage and with confidence. Our intention is a simple one: more effective teaching.

Trevor Kerry, series editor
2002

How to use this book

This teaching skills series of books is designed to fulfil two closely related but not identical intentions for teachers in training, newly qualified teachers, and others who want to examine their practice more closely. The first is to help you become a 'thinking teacher', and the second is to encourage reflective practice.

The literature of continuing professional development for teachers and managers is full of references to reflective practice. The point of this approach is that the professional – in whatever role – is able to stand aside from himself or herself and to take an objective look at their own behaviour and actions as well as those of others. From this objective approach he or she can learn – can reflect upon practice – and can mould behaviour to be more productive.

To be a 'thinking teacher' is slightly different. It implies that you have a curious mind: one that questions, is open to ideas and change, that investigates problems rather than accepts the solutions of others, and that sustains a degree of intellectualism in all that you do. This approach is, after all, what you are trying to encourage in your pupils. This is something that is highlighted in Hay McBer's (2000) Report as one of the professional characteristics, or what it calls 'deep-seated patterns of behaviour'.

To achieve these ends, the books in the series are closely modelled on the requirements for teachers as drawn together in two crucial pieces of official literature: the Hay McBer Report (2000) already mentioned: a Report commissioned by the Government to draw together aspects of good practice in teaching; and the Teacher Training Agency's (TTA) National Standards for Qualified Teacher Status.

Within the books, each chapter is constructed so as to:

- Indicate the learning about the specific teaching skill that is outlined in the chapter
- Provide suitable text, with illustrations and examples, to carry the reader through the learning process
- Include useful checklists, Tables and Figures to break up the text and to serve as *aide-memoires*
- Invite participation in learning through Activities designed to improve your skills
- Summarise the key learning points at the end of each chapter.

It is important to stress that the material is all real. By that is meant that every classroom example has been used in, and culled from, an actual classroom where the activity reported was used successfully. There are no fictional examples. Furthermore, the material in the chapters has all been put to use in national training courses that have run successfully and been repeated several times: it is tried and tested material that has received professional approval. In the same way, all the Activities have been used by teachers, though that is not to say that every Activity would be equally practical or feasible in every school.

It is also imperative to point out that teaching skills, and the thinking that underpins them, are not free from controversy or debate. Indeed, part of the professionalism referred to by Hay McBer is to engage in precisely those debates. Thus the reader must not assume when reading the books in this series that he or she will not be challenged to engage in that debate at times: it would be a mistake if this were not the case. Nevertheless, the authors of this series, experts in their fields, have not peppered its pages with academic references; these last are used sparingly so as not to interrupt the flow of the text.

This, and the other books in the series, are designed to take the reader on from knowledge to skill in an interactive way, through using the Activities and through trying out ideas in the practitioner's own classroom. Some people will find the learning process easier if they maintain a reflective log, however brief, or use a tape recorder to play back parts of their lessons for later analysis, or work with a colleague who can observe them and give feedback (team working is favoured by both Hay McBer and the National Standards documents).

In practice the books can each be used in a variety of ways:

- As a continuous text: the reader then just reads over the Activities as they arise
- As a training manual: in which the reader pauses at the Activities and tries them out
- As a source book: the reader can dip into specific sections for particular help and guidance.

Similarly, the context in which the texts can be used will vary. In many instances, a book will simply be read as a text for self-development by a teacher working alone. In other cases, a school may adopt the title as part of its in-house training programme, and colleagues will discuss and share its text and Activities as on-going professional development. There will be some who use the text as part of training conferences or lectures. The material should prove invaluable to teachers in training and as a support for teaching practice. The outline of skills in each title may also be adapted by heads, and others who act as appraisers, as a guide to their observation of, and feedback to, colleagues.

These are books about what happens 'at the sharp end' – in the classroom.

Key references

Department for Education and Skills (2001) *Schools achieving success*. London: DfES.

Department for Education and Skills (2002) *Education and Skills: Delivering Results – a strategy to 2006*. London: DfES.

Hay McBer (2000) *Research into Teacher Effectiveness*. Report by Hay McBer to the Department for Education and Employment, June 2000.

Teacher Training Agency (2001) *Standards for the Award of Qualified Teacher Status*. London: TTA.

Teacher Training Agency (2002) *Qualifying to Teach*. London: TTA.

Note

TTA (2001) was produced as a consultation document. It contained two sections – the National Standards (statutory) and the Handbook (non-statutory guidance). Following the consultation period there was considerable objection to the Handbook element as being too prescriptive. The decision was made, we understand, by TTA to rewrite this latter element. At the time of compiling this book only the statutory Standards had been revised – TTA (2002) – also referred to in the text as QTT. This was a fairly superficial document, lacking as it was a version of the Handbook from TTA (2001). For this reason, and because we believed that the original Handbook gave important clues to the way that government thinking was working – which might operate during inspections, for example – we have chosen to retain reference to this document as the Draft Handbook. The updated version of the Handbook, promised for Spring 2002 by the TTA, was still not available in June as this text went to press.

PART ONE

EXPLANATIONS AND EXPLAINING

TEACHERS TALKING

1

OBJECTIVES

This chapter invites you:

- To review what the National Standards say about teachers as explainers
- To compare and contrast 'better' and 'worse' explanations
- To begin to explore explaining skills.

INTRODUCTION: NATIONAL STANDARDS AND EXPLAINING

It is perhaps odd, and certainly anachronistic, that teaching and talking (by which, of course, is implied 'explaining') are viewed as virtually synonymous. It is this failure to make distinctions that lies behind Hay McBer's opening comments (para 1.2.4) in the section 'Teaching Skills Described'.

> *The effective teachers whom we observed ... were actively involved with their pupils at all times. Many of the activities were teacher-led ...*

And later:

> *So what we saw effective teachers doing was a great deal of instruction to whole classes ... But the active style of teaching does not result in passive pupils ...*

Of course, an emphasis on the skill of explaining is inevitable in a curriculum that is content led in the way that the National Curriculum is, and also in any curriculum that is prescribed and then assessed assiduously. That is not to deny that 'talking' is – and always has been – an important teaching skill. Indeed, in the new climate of learning support, where support staff deal with individual pupils and small groups, that same skill is important for them as much as for the teacher.

To elaborate this latter point, we were researching recently in a school where support staff were used as learning mentors for GCSE pupils. One pupil informed us solemnly that the advantage of this system was that 'the mentor explains things more clearly than the teacher'. Intrigued, we followed up this comment. Was that a generalisation, or was there a specific example of where this had happened in relation to a particular lesson? No; teachers made content complicated, and mentors made it easy! So make no mistake: we all need to explain more clearly, more precisely, and more engagingly the things that we wish to communicate to pupils, while both teachers and learning support staff need to read this section on explaining and acquire the skills.

The Draft Handbook (TTA 2001) put proper emphasis on teacher talk. This is not the place to revisit what the Draft Handbook says, relevantly and crucially, about such issues as planning and setting learning objectives (e.g. paras 3.1.2 and 3.1.3). These are dealt with in a companion volume in this series, though the messages apply to lessons based on explaining and are implicit throughout this text. In the same way, para 3.2.2 implies teacher explanations as at least one approach towards teachers teaching:

> *... the required or expected knowledge, understanding and skills relevant to the curriculum for pupils in the age range for which they are trained ...*

This knowledge, of course, is related to either Key Stage 2 (cross-curricular) or Key Stage 3 (specialist subjects and the relevant national frameworks). However, it is at para 3.2.5 that the Draft Handbook makes specific reference to the core skills in Part One of this text. Here we read that teachers must:

> *Teach clearly structured lessons, or sequences of work, which make learning objectives clear to pupils ...*

These requirements include lessons that involve:

- clear introductions which capture interest, link to previous learning and explain what is to be learned;
- use of a range of clear and stimulating strategies to secure motivation and concentration;
- examples to help pupils learn concepts;
- links between one piece of learning and its generalisation to other settings and problems.

Draft Handbook para 3.2.5 indicates that to achieve these ends teachers must use a range of techniques, namely:

- directing and telling
- demonstrating and modelling
- explaining and illustrating
- discussing and questioning
- exploring and investigating
- consolidating and embedding
- checking regularly for understanding
- summarising and reviewing
- reflecting and evaluating
- using humour, narrative, games and action.

In addition, pupils must be taught (Draft Handbook para 3.2.7) to:

- link new learning to what they already know

- make connections, generalisations and construct rules, and
- express and clarify their ideas and opinions
- generate and test hypotheses
- imagine and empathise
- critically respond and evaluate.

These are all skills covered in this text, in one or both parts. But we should not lose sight of the fact that these targets can be achieved only if they are underpinned by that other important teacher skill – the ability to create an appropriate learning ethos; a skill acknowledged in para 3.4.2 of the same source, where teachers must be able to:

> *Establish an ethos with the class or groups they teach which values diversity, acknowledges pupils' strengths and promotes success.*

The context of the Draft Handbook, and thus of the teaching skills contained in them, was the Government's drive to raise standards. It is, therefore, regrettable that QTT (TTA 2002) – the Government's latest publication – is virtually silent on these critical areas of teaching skill. Everything that is said in these present manuals is intended to improve teaching with a view to improving learning. Whether this is best achieved and measured by means of standardised tests is a debate that the profession needs to have with itself and with government – but the national aspirations are clear, and can be accessed in the White Paper (2001) and in the document Education and Skills (DfES 2002) which are included in the Key References on page xi.

Teachers spend a lot of time talking. This simple statement forms the backdrop to much that is said in this book. Later, in Chapter 8, we discuss some of the research into teacher talk, and the theories about learning which are derived from it. In what follows it is the intention to move directly into the relevant skills required of the teacher when talk is in the form of explanation.

If we were to eavesdrop on a typical lesson in almost any primary or secondary school it would be rare to find it begin in any other way than with the teacher talking through some kind of introduction. This has been noted earlier in the book – even in the context of question-based lessons. There is a strong psychological compulsion to begin any group activity with a shared experience, even if this is only a brief recapitulation of what has gone before.

In practice, this brief recap is almost certainly going to be augmented in a moment or two by some new input to the theme by the teacher: addressed to all students, a group or simply an individual to aid understanding. Then there may well be some instructions to students about the task which the teacher intends to set them. The teacher talk and the instructions are both forms of explanation. It is with these aspects of teaching skill that the first half of this book deals. Explanations may be punctuated or followed by questions – and appropriate reference should be made to later chapters.

So, let's imagine we have dropped in on lessons in two parallel classes. Both the classes are going to make study visits – it could be in any curriculum area – and both are going to compile a record of some of their learning using simple cameras. In each class the teacher is giving an explanation about how the camera works. What we hear is the two explanations below. Your task is to read the explanations and then carry out Activity 1.

Better or worse? No 1

How to get the most from a simple camera

'Now this [holds up camera and waves it about] is an Instamatic. It is dead easy to operate because it doesn't need any setting: all you have to do is point and shoot. It's the proverbial black box, really; all the works go on without you having to bother with it.

'So what you need to do is to point it at something you want to photograph, and then press the button here [demonstrates the shutter release]. Of course, you have to look through the viewfinder first and line up the shot – Auntie Mabel or whatever – and then press.

'When you've done that, send the film off for processing in one of those little envelopes you get in Radio Times sometimes; or take it to Boots – they're pretty good value, and quick. That's why it's called an Instamatic really.'

Better or worse? No 2

The Instamatic revisited

'Today we are going to learn how to work this camera [passes it round the group], and how to get the most from it. There are three basic things we need to learn: first, how to load a film; second, how to take a satisfying picture and third, how to operate the camera.

'Let's look at each of these in turn.

'So, first, loading a film.

'Instamatic film comes in a closed plastic container called a cassette, like this [shows one]. The film has a note on it [here, look] saying: "this way up". So the steps in loading are:

- lay the camera face down on a non-abrasive surface so as not to scratch the lens
- keep the film up the right way, as marked
- pull down on this catch on the camera body [demonstrates: back pops open]
- slot the film in
- close the back [demonstrates], and listen for the "whirr" that shows it's wound on.

'Now, we are ready to take some pictures. So how do we go about that? Well . . .

'Hold the camera to your eye like this [shows].

'You do it, Sam. Thank you. What do you see? Yes, you get a picture of the corner of the classroom, and you can move around to frame it better, include more people, use a low or high angle for effect ... we can come back to those skills later.

'So, thirdly, let's look at what we call "taking the picture". On the top of the camera, by your index finger, is a button called the shutter release. To take the picture you squeeze; that's important because a jerky movement may shake the camera and give you a fuzzy picture ...'

Activity 1

Looking for quality in explanations

Having read the two versions of the explanation about using an instamatic camera (above), identify which one you thought was better.

Now make a list of the criteria which you used to come to that judgement.

You might now want to revisit the better explanation, and to ask yourself what could have been done to improve it.

What follows in the rest of this book is a closer examination of what explaining is, and how it can be carried out more effectively. But before we move on to these, it is opportune to spend the rest of this chapter in setting the scene for why explaining skills are important to teachers.

Clearly, we have said that teachers spend a lot of time explaining things to students. The very volume of explanation in classrooms makes it critical that it should be done well. Explanation is a fundamental skill of communication: and teaching is a profession of communicators. Yet we have to admit that our skills are often not as good as those of others in the communications business: those who work in the news and the media, those who write advertisements and sell products, even some politicians, are slicker at explaining things than we are!

I have tried, over the years, to probe why teachers do not always exhibit the highest levels of skills in explaining, and why – though they explain for a living – they do not always feel confident doing it. The paragraphs which follow give an account of one of the ways I have used, in professional development sessions on explaining skills, to highlight the issue:

> *Following the keynote lecture, delegates were divided into groups, each with a group leader. Group leaders had been briefed prior to the training day. This workshop looked to put into practice some of the messages and strategies conveyed in the keynote talk.*
>
> *Each leader was given an envelope containing a series of titles based on everyday events or activities. Delegates were asked to select a title 'blind' – they then had ten minutes in which to prepare a two-minute explanation on the theme selected.*
>
> *One person from the group was selected to give their explanation;*

other delegates in the group acted as audience or as recorders (the latter listened to the explanation and rated it on criteria previously supplied). Then delegates changed roles, and listened to the next explanation, and so on . . .

At the end of the session, the group leader was asked to spend a few minutes collecting the thoughts and feelings of the delegates about the exercise.

This apparently innocuous exercise proves to be a quite traumatic experience for many teachers: even for those who had spent many years explaining in front of literally hundreds of classes. Why? What do they say about their experience?

Asked about how they feel when giving their mini-explanations, here are some of the responses:

'There was a tendency to think I had less time than was available in reality.'

'The session proved how much one needs to prepare.'

'It was very difficult to work with a peer (as opposed to a student) group.'

'I would have preferred to share ideas before giving the explanation.'

'Knowledge of the audience is important, and I did not know all the members of my group.'

'The stress level was very high today.'

'How can I cope with audience disaffection?'

You may be surprised by some of these statements. What they demonstrate is a diffidence not usually associated with teachers! Perhaps part of the reason for this is that, when a skill comes under the spotlight or is transferred to a new context, instinctive or habitual patterns of behaviour suddenly seem to desert the victim: we simply don't question our behaviours enough in the normal course of events.

In this exercise the delegates were also asked to spend some time playing the role of listeners, i.e. of students. What they had to say about this is equally interesting:

'It is very hard to concentrate on things that have nothing to do with one's own experience.'

'I needed someone to capture my interest.'

Could the reality be that students feel like this a lot of the time? Of course, we hardly like to admit it; but there is quite a bit of evidence that it is the case.

Activity 2

Following a class

Try to negotiate a day or half a day when you can be freed from teaching (perhaps as part of your appraisal outcome or by use of INSET monies or when you are team teaching).

Use the time to follow a class. Simply attend all the sessions they attend and, within reason, do what they are asked to do. How easy did you find it to:

- concentrate
- understand difficult lessons
- sustain enthusiasm across the curriculum
- listen for a sustained period?

Has this exercise given you more empathy with the students?

So, even in a situation which requires such a basic teaching skill as explaining, teachers may feel diffident and lack confidence; students may feel bored, out of their depth, or even disaffected. But what of the teacher-delegates to our conference on explaining? What were their reflections on the process of explaining itself? This is what they said about giving their two-minute mini-explanations:

> *'One needs to know and have confidence in the subject matter.'*
>
> *'It is important to know, or be able to research, the subject matter.'*
>
> *'One needs a relaxed atmosphere in which to perform well.'*
>
> *'Careful layout of the room is necessary to keep eye-contact.'*
>
> *'One needs to think through even the simplest operations in a clear, logical order.'*
>
> *'One must enhance the talk with visual aids.'*
>
> *'It is easy to assume too much of your audience.'*
>
> *'Humour adds an extra dimension.'*
>
> *'Pace and pauses are important.'*
>
> *'Keep to the time limits.'*
>
> *'Personal experience may bring an explanation alive, but one must take care not to stray from the topic.'*
>
> *'During a long explanation, effective interaction is needed.'*
>
> *'Above all, make sure that what you are saying is worth saying.'*

In this last section of comment there is a move towards identifying some of the skills of an effective explainer: to these we shall return systematically in later chapters. For the moment let us concentrate on two matters. The first is that the exercise described revealed a degree of vulnerability by the teachers involved, which some might find a little surprising. The second is that explaining must be, by definition, the paramount skill in didactic teaching methods, and we must pay some attention to these before we proceed.

Despite this book's later emphasis on questioning skills no one who reads the education press can doubt that there has been considerable pressure to revert to what are seen as the halcyon days of students sitting in rows with teachers talking at them. This didactic approach, it is believed, had great merits which were somehow lost to sight when students were more involved in lessons, discovered things for themselves, and were cognitively challenged. It signals a return to an earlier era, as Bourne – in an historical review of practice (1994) – notes:

> *A streamed class was supposed to contain children of a similar 'ability' (or intelligence). It was theoretically (or intellectually) respectable, therefore, to continue to rely on whole class teaching as the main approach, and this also, of course, allowed a further lease of life to didacticism ... In other words, during these 20 post-war years, the situation became crystallised. (p. 12)*

The logic of the argument in favour of this view may not be entirely clear to you (or to me): but the view exists. The result is that teachers are expected to spend a significant amount of classroom time in didactic methods. A more logical view might be that promulgated by Bennett, in a review of primary practice in which he points out the difficulties of identifying teaching styles:

> *Another problem was the large between-style differences. For example, although, on average, formal styles related better to progress, some formal teachers were able to generate much better progress than other formal teachers. Similarly, some informal teachers were successful, but others much less so. In other words, teaching style in itself did not, and could not, provide an adequate explanation of differences in pupil outcomes.*
>
> (Bennett in Cullingford, C. (ed.) (1997) *The Politics of Primary Education*. Milton Keynes: Open University Press, p. 127)

While we can debate the merits of didactic methods, and argue about how much time is appropriate to be spent on them, the fact is that didactic teaching is one fundamental teaching method: and explaining skills lie at the heart of it. So whether an individual teacher does more or less of it is irrelevant: all teachers do some didactic work, and they have to be good at the explaining skills which underpin it.

A note on Activity 1, on page 7

The second explanation is preferred, because, among other things, it is clearer, better sequenced, better structured, based on examples, and it uses language better to emphasise its key points.

Outcomes

At the end of this chapter you should have:

- Learned what is required of teachers as explainers
- Considered criteria for judging the quality of explanations, including your own
- Looked at explanations from the pupils' point of view
- Opened a discussion with yourself about the role of didactic teaching.

2 How explanations work

OBJECTIVES

This chapter invites you:

- To consider the elements in an explanation
- To examine three different types of explanation
- To see how an explanation is constructed to make teaching points.

Every explanation involves three elements: an explainer, explainees, and something to be explained. Or, to put it another way: a teacher, one or more students, and the subject matter.

It is quite possible that – in any given explanation – a bias can be imparted according to which of these three elements is seen as most important. For example, if a teacher thinks that their act of giving the explanation lies at the heart of the process, then there will be most concentration given to crafting that explanation, to the skills of being an explainer – such as choosing exactly the right words and presenting the information in exactly the right order.

By contrast, from the students' perspective, it may be that what they are looking for as explainees is the sustaining of interest: they may value the use of examples, or of humour to add interest to the process – since they do have to endure it for many hours each day.

However, if the subject matter itself is seen as the heart of the explaining process, then the content will be viewed as more important than either the craft of the explainer or the involvement of the explainees. For me, this bias was most vividly illustrated in a conversation with a tutor in a university Law department. We were discussing the merits of improving explaining skills; but he rejected the notion. I asked him on what grounds he felt this was justified. 'Well,' he replied, 'as far as we are concerned we only have to tell our students about all the cases relevant to the topic, and all they have to do is remember them. Everything else is window-dressing.'

I have laboured this point about differing perspectives only in order to say that all three are important, and that all three will be covered in this book.

So, what exactly is explaining? The best answer is given, in my view, by Brown and Hatton (1982): explaining is giving understanding to another person. We need to note at the outset that the giving is not merely of information, but of that more cognitively demanding element: understanding.

In this chapter we shall go on to look at different kinds of explanation, before considering in the next how to deliver these effectively to a student audience.

Most classroom explanations fall into one of three categories. They answer implicit questions:

- What? questions
- How? questions
- Why? questions.

WHAT? QUESTIONS: INTERPRETATIVE EXPLANATIONS

- What is climate?
- What is a graph?
- What do we mean by evidence?
- What is migration?
- What are the characteristics of a good story?
- What are the possible routes from A to B?
- What is a 'testudo'?

When we give explanations to student groups we are usually dealing with implicit questions such as those listed above. We have decided that, rather than posing the question to the students and sending them off to discover the answers from texts and resources, we will deliver the information orally to everyone at once.

Explanation is often used precisely for this reason: to save time and energy by delivering basic knowledge to a group in the most economical way. Indeed, that is why didactic teaching finds such support with politicians and with those educationists whose overriding concern rests more in financial economies than in intellectual engagement. But it is a legitimate enough way to proceed for at least some classroom time. Its main merit is that it provides the shared platform of information and experience which was discussed in the previous chapter.

HOW? QUESTIONS: DESCRIPTIVE EXPLANATIONS

- How does climate change across Britain?
- How can we construct a graph about our TV viewing habits?
- How can we find evidence about this topic?
- How do birds migrate?
- How can we best write our own short story?
- How can we get from A to B most cheaply?
- How did the Romans form the 'testudo'?

These explanations deal with structures, processes or procedures. They are about the mechanisms by which things work. As such, they form the background to much classroom work.

WHY? QUESTIONS: REASON-GIVING EXPLANATIONS

- Why does the climate change as we travel from West to East?
- Why is the graph a useful tool?
- Why is evidence so essential to historians?
- Why do birds migrate?
- Why is this short story a successful example?
- Why is the route we have chosen from A to B the best?
- Why was the 'testudo' so effective?

Earlier, we noted that explaining was 'giving understanding to another'. In this cognitive process, explanations which answer implicit 'Why?' questions are especially significant. They unlock the door to understanding about how things work, why they are successful. They identify:

- reasons
- causes
- motivations, and
- justifications for ideas or behaviours.

Before you read on, Activity 3 gives you the opportunity to examine your own use of explanation.

Activity 3

Exploring your own use of explanations

Which kinds of explanations do you use? To find out tape-record a sample of your lessons (just the portions where you are giving explanations will suffice).

Later, go over the tapes and identify which of three types of explanation you have used, and how often. You can record the outcomes on a table like this:

	Interpretative	Descriptive	Reason-giving
	✓✓✓	✓✓	✓✓
Total:	3	2	2

Use the same tapes to make an assessment of whether you think your explanations concentrate more upon your techniques as an explainer, the students' understanding, or the subject matter – or is the balance about right?

Use the results from this Activity to ask yourself what it tells you about your 'explaining style'.

Now you have had a chance to review your own use of explanations, let us return to the theme of types of explanation. It may be helpful to illustrate this by taking one of the examples of subject matter listed above, and following it through all three types of explanation:

- What is a 'testudo'?

- How was a testudo formed?
- Why was the testudo so effective?

These explanations would relate to a history lesson on Roman Britain, perhaps at Key Stage 2. The resulting explanation by the teacher might go something like this:

Testudo!

'In your reading of this page some of you have come across a strange word: testudo. I want everyone to pause while I explain what a testudo is. "Testudo" is a Latin word – you remember Latin was the language spoken by the Romans whom we are studying. The word means "tortoise". But you can see from what you have read that the Romans didn't carry tortoises into battle with them. However, the commander might have shouted something like: Form a tortoise!

'The testudo was a shape, like a tortoise, made with shields. If you look at the school tortoise you can see it has a hard shell, and the shell has marks and ridges on it as if it is made from flat plates. What the Romans did was to use a tortoise-like shell of shields to protect the men inside as they went into battle.

'To make the testudo, or tortoise shell, the men had to be drawn up in a square or a rectangle. About eight men would stand side by side; and exactly behind them another eight, and so on – maybe ten rows of men, one behind the other. When the order "Form tortoise!" was given, the men in the front row all held their shields in front of them. The men in the back row held their shields behind them. The men in the right of the group held their shields on their right arms to protect the right side of the column; and the men on the left held their shields on the left in the same way.

'Now, it didn't matter whether the enemy threw spears or stones at them from the side, the front or the back, all the men were protected. However, there was more to it than that. The idea of this rectangular column was to march right up to the gates of the enemy's fort and knock them down. As they got close to the gates and the walls of the fort, the enemy could throw things down on their heads. So the men in the column who were on the inner ranks, protected front and rear, left and right, put their shields over their heads and the heads of the other soldiers, like a lid. Now they were shut into a tortoise shell. The enemy could throw things from front, side, back or on top without damaging the men in the testudo. They could advance right up to the fort, smash open the door, and rush in to attack.

'There were two main reasons why the testudo was so successful as a tactic. The first was because of the nature of the fighting that often took place. At that time, the native Britons had not built big, stone castles like we see sometimes today. The forts were usually built quite quickly, wherever an army was. They probably built them on a hillside so that the attackers had to run uphill and were slowed up. But they were probably made of wooden posts, with wooden gateways. The people inside would fire arrows from the top of the low wooden walls at the distant enemy; and when they got closer would drop missiles on top of them. So the attackers had to stay protected from these missiles for long enough to break down the gates of the fort. The testudo meant the Romans could do just that. This became a very important reason why the Romans could usually win in battles with the Britons.

'The second reason for its success had to do with the shape of the shield: it was not round like the native Britons' shields, but rectangular. It was also curved inwards. When several shields were locked together, then, they formed protection around the body: and there were no gaps through which missiles or hot liquids could be thrown.'

Activity 4

Spotting the transition between types of explanation

Read over the explanation 'Testudo' (above).

Identify the points at which the explanation changes from interpretative to descriptive, and from descriptive to reason-giving.

The explanation used in the example above contains all three elements: interpretative, descriptive and reason-giving. Of course, in the real world, it may not have looked exactly like the text quoted here. For example:

- the three elements may have been separated, and given on different occasions or in different parts of the lesson;
- the teacher may have punctuated the explanation with questions to the students;
- the teacher may have used these questions either to check on understanding or to set a further problem for the students to investigate;
- the teacher may have used visual aids – perhaps if this explanation was a main part of the lesson (as opposed to arising spontaneously), she may have brought along pre-prepared visual aids, and so on.

So, this example is not meant to be an exemplar of perfect explaining (it contains strengths and weaknesses); but it is the kind of spontaneous explanation that teachers are called on to give every day.

Nevertheless, though this example is not meant to be perfect, it is opportune to draw attention to a very important feature of it, and one which is vital to every good explanation: sequencing. The absolutely fundamental skill of every explainer has to be to sequence material effectively, and deal with the elements in the explanation in the correct order.

In this context Testudo! will repay another examination, using Activity 5.

Activity 5

Sequencing an explanation

Read back over Testudo!

List the main points of the explanation as a series of short statements, for example, Testudo means 'tortoise', it was a shape like a tortoise, it was made by shields, etc.

Note how the material in it is presented in a logical order.

Having established that explanations are designed to promote understanding, that they serve a variety of purposes, and that the *sine qua non* of the successful explanation is correct sequencing of the material within it, we are ready to move on in the next chapter to look more systematically at some other important elements that go into making an explanation effective.

Outcomes

At the end of this chapter you should have:

- Understood the different kinds of explanation that are commonly used
- Learned how to analyse explanations into these three types
- Begun to have thought analytically about sequencing material in an explanation.

3 Explaining in practice

OBJECTIVES

This chapter invites you:

- To formulate strategies for making explanations more effective
- To plan an explanation with these strategies in mind
- To examine explanations for 'key elements' that may be missing
- To visit some explaining skills in outline.

In the previous chapters we have looked at what an explanation is, and have explored in an informal way what makes one explanation better or worse than another. In this section we start to look more systematically at composing explanations using deliberate strategies to make them effective.

The place to begin is with the content of the materials we want to teach. Let us imagine that we want to teach a piece of science curriculum: let's say the concept of holding territory. The first job is to begin to put together the key ideas that need to be communicated. In the first instance, when planning explanations, it is often useful to make some notes. Our notes might look like this:

TERRITORY: notes

Key ideas:

- What is territory?
- How is territory recognised?
- Why is territory important?

Key ideas revisited:

1 What is territory?
- definition needed
- examples from students' experience

2 How is territory recognised?
- by other creatures of similar kind
- by us
- territory marking
- testing out the information

3 Why is territory important?
- food
- attracting a mate
- breeding success
- survival.

This outline plan would certainly do as a first attempt. Notice that it uses the framework from the previous chapter in that it asks the three key questions which distinguish types of explanation, but which – as we have said – often merge together in practice. At this stage it would be possible to use this outline to draft the text of an explanation, as in Activity 6.

Activity 6

Drafting an explanation

If you feel *au fait* enough with the subject matter (or are prepared to do a little research) try drafting your explanation based on the notes on Territory.

When you have done this compare your draft with the one given below. What are the differences? Keep the notes to refer to as the chapter proceeds.

Territory One

'Today we are going to look at an important occurrence in the animal world: holding a territory. But first we have to think about what the word territory means.

'Territory is a space, a piece of land if you like, in which an animal lives, and over which it has ownership.

'You can see this at work in the gardens around the school whenever you look out of the window at this time of year. You may have noticed the blackbirds: they sit up on the roofs and the TV aerials and sing. Every so often they move to another spot and sing again. If you were to draw a map of this immediate area, and to watch where the bird sang from, and then were to mark on the map those points the bird sang from, you would have mapped its territory – the space within which it lives.

'Now, if you own a piece of territory, you want to mark it out as yours. When we own a house we often put up a fence or plant a hedge to mark out the boundaries. That fence or hedge borders the territory: it's a sort of signal to others that this is ours, so keep off! Some land-owners put up signs: "Private – keep out" or "Trespassers will be prosecuted". Birds and animals do much the same. Of course, the blackbird doesn't put up a fence, but the fence is still there: other blackbirds know it is. They know that the ground between the first bird's song-posts is already occupied. Other animals use methods to mark their territory: birds sing, but many mammals use scent. They do exactly what the blackbird does, and wander around the edges of their space; but as they go they leave traces of scent from glands, often near the tail, or they urinate, which serves the same purpose.

'The reasons animals hold territories are several. First, if they own a space they can more easily guarantee a food supply. Then, with a nice pad to live in, the male might attract a female more easily. Once he has attracted a mate, he can breed – and if it's a good territory with plenty of food the young will probably stay alive. So, in the longer term the species will survive.

This first attempt at an explanation on territory, Territory One, can serve as a useful vehicle for us to analyse with a view to identifying some further skills of explaining. So before reading on, tackle Activity 7.

Activity 7

Finding what is missing from an explanation

We have already indicated that this explanation contains a sensitivity to the three kinds of explaining described in Chapter 2: interpretative, descriptive and reason-giving.

The task now is to start to examine the explanation for what is missing. Read over the explanation several times and try to suggest ways in which its presentation could be improved. Here are one or two clues to start you off. Add your own criteria to the list:

- clarity of language
- use of examples
- pace.

The next step, then, is to look at our explanation, Territory One, section by section, and to try to identify factors which would improve its effectiveness.

> *Today we are going to look at an important occurrence in the animal world: holding a territory. But first we have to think about what the word territory means.*
>
> *Territory is a space, a piece of land if you like, in which an animal lives, and over which it has ownership.*

This is quite an effective introduction to the explanation. It has two merits: first, it lets the students know what is on the learning agenda; and second, it attempts to answer the What? question by positing a simple definition. The definition itself offers two 'models' (space, piece of land) which students can visualise. The concept of ownership is important to the definition, too.

Could the introduction have been improved? Possibly – though we have to bear in mind there is no such thing as the 'perfect lesson', so there are no right answers here. It may have been improved by watching the blackbird outside the window for a while first – to explore behaviour observed by, and thus known to be in the experience of, all the students.

Thus, the next section of the explanation begins, appropriately enough, with a link to what *may* be the students' experience.

> *You can see this at work in the gardens around the school whenever you look out of the window at this time of year. You may have noticed the blackbirds: they sit up on the roofs and the TV aerials and sing. Every so often they move to another spot and sing again. If you were to draw a map of this immediate area, and to watch where the bird sang from, and then were to mark on the map those points the bird sang from, you would have mapped its territory – the space within which it lives.*

This segment of the explanation is mainly an extended example. The use of examples is certainly to be commended: more than one example is often needed to establish a rule or pattern that the students can take away from the explanation. The use of both positive and negative examples is also helpful: 'It works like this ... but not like this ...'. The whole paragraph would have been more powerful, of course, if the students had actually carried out the operation described; but the teacher has to make a professional judgement about when it is, and when it is not, appropriate to spend time in this way.

> *Now, if you own a piece of territory, you want to mark it out as yours. When we own a house we often put up a fence or plant a hedge to mark out the boundaries. That fence or hedge borders the territory: it's a sort of signal to others that this is ours, so keep off! Some landowners put up signs: 'Private – keep out' or 'Trespassers will be prosecuted'. Birds and animals do much the same. Of course, the blackbird doesn't put up a fence, but the fence is still there: other blackbirds know it is. They know that the ground between the first bird's song-posts is already occupied.*

The explanation continues with a second example. This taps into the known – what happens around human dwellings – and so reinforces the concept of territory. It doesn't pause to draw attention to the newly introduced concept of 'song-post'; but it adds a degree of extra clarity, and some emphasis to what has gone before. This done, the explanation moves on to a new idea:

> *Other animals use different methods to mark their territory: birds sing, but many mammals use scent. They do exactly what the blackbird does, and wander around the edges of their space; but as they go they leave traces of scent from glands, often near the tail, or they urinate, which serves the same purpose.*

The teacher now extends the concept from blackbirds to mammals, repeating the general rule or principle, but adding a couple of other ways in which it operates in the wild. The explanation has moved on quite logically from a definition, through examples, to generalisation and the establishment of the principle of territory.

However, we have noted a lack of concrete experience, and a dearth of visual stimuli to drive home the learning. The other missing feature of this explanation is that we get no real feel for the use of 'connectives' in the language to help continuity (however, then, although, consequently, etc.). Note how most sentences start straight in with statements: 'Other animals ...'; 'They do exactly ...'. The sequence of the explanation is clear; but opportunities are lost to make links through these linguistic ploys. There are no signals that any point is more significant than any other, nor any use of repetition of words, thoughts or ideas to give specific emphasis. So the explanation continues:

> ***The reasons animals hold territories are several. First, if they own a space they can more easily guarantee a food supply. Then, with a nice pad to live in, the male might attract a female more easily. Once he has attracted a mate, he can breed – and if it's a good territory with plenty of food the young will probably stay alive. So, in the longer term the species will survive.***

This last segment of the explanation has several points of note. The first is that the pace suddenly changes: it actually gets quite a lot faster. While it has taken some longish paragraphs to explain the basic concept of territory, the list of reasons why this is important is dashed off in a handful of sentences. Beginning with 'First, if ...' implies there will be 'numbered points' – but these fade out after the first one, or perhaps after 'Then ...' (meaning secondly). By contrast, there is a connective in the last sentence: 'So'. There is also the use of a semi-humorous expression: '... with a nice pad to live in ...'.

The next point to note about this last segment of the explanation is that once again a new technical term has been introduced (perhaps for the first time to these students), and without definition or explanation: survival. This leads us to deduce that perhaps there are other technical terms or concepts which might have been included appropriately into this explanation. For example, the concept of territory needs to be distinguished from another that the youngsters will need to know in this curriculum area: habitat. Finally, what is missing totally from this explanation is the 'feedback loop': how does the teacher know whether the students are following and understanding this explanation?

So, what have we learned from this analysis of a real classroom explanation? By going back over the analysis we can see that what emerges is a list of skills required of an explainer. Try doing this in Activity 8.

Activity 8

Deducing the skills of explaining

Read back over the section of the chapter from Activity 7.

Use your notes from Activity 7, and your re-reading, to compile as full a list of explaining skills as you can identify.

Compare your list with the one which follows.

When you have done that, move on to the next chapter, where these skills are discussed in more detail.

Explaining skills deduced from the Territory One text:

1 Thinking of a dynamic introduction.
2 Defining the key terms or concepts.
3 Linking the explanation with concrete experience.
4 Using examples: both positive and negative.
5 Building in tasks.
6 Introducing and using technical language.
7 Developing rules and principles.
8 Using connectives efficiently to enhance meaning.
9 Exploiting 'linguistic ploys'.
10 Using repetition and emphasis.
11 Adopting an appropriate pace.
12 'Numbering' points.
13 Using humour.
14 Linking the explanation to other knowledge.
15 Building in the 'feedback loop'.

Outcomes

At the end of this chapter you should have:

- Understood the structure of an explanation
- Planned an explanation using this understanding
- Deduced some important skills of explaining.

---

4 FIFTEEN SKILLS FOR EXPLAINERS

OBJECTIVES

This chapter invites you:

- To revisit the fifteen skills for explainers outlined in Chapter 3
- To consider each skill individually and in practice in classrooms
- To relate the skills, where relevant, to the National Standards
- To take an overview of the skills working together, using a lesson transcript.

In this chapter we are going to work through the fifteen skills for explainers which have been deduced from the example Territory One quoted in the previous chapter.

1 THINKING OF A DYNAMIC INTRODUCTION

The advice that has often been given to beginning teachers about lessons is: Start with a bang not a whimper. This is good advice, and it probably applies equally to explanations within a lesson as well as to whole lessons. Of course, not every lesson can – nor probably should – start with metaphorical fireworks; the aim is a more modest capturing of the imagination.

Explanations often come near the beginning of lessons; so it is especially important when explaining to make a positive start. Attention has to be captured: the ultimate understanding of the explanation depends on students following carefully the steps you are going to outline, so it is important not to lose the attention of the students at the very start.

Many explanations begin, in practice, with a recap of what went on in a previous session: this provides the 'shared experience' to which reference was made earlier – a phenomenon with which teachers feel safe. But a recap rarely provides a dynamic starting point. So perhaps the answer is to separate the recap from the start of the explanation of new material.

Later in the book (see pages 92–94) there is a discussion of how the recap itself can be made more varied: for the moment we will assume that it takes the most basic form of one or two revision questions, and the students' responses to them. What follows is a fairly typical lesson beginning:

T: Who can remember what we were talking about last time?
S1: Food chains, Miss.

T: Correct. So who can give me an example of a food chain? David?
S2: A hoverfly feeds off a plant; a dragonfly eats the hoverfly; the dragonfly is caught by a small bird; the small bird is eaten by a sparrowhawk.
T: Yes – that's the general idea. OK, well today we're going on to look at another aspect of the behaviour of living things. It's called Territory . . .

As an introduction, this has served the basic purposes; but it is prosaic at best. It doesn't grab attention, and the links between the two pieces of work are not well made. Could it have been better? Perhaps this dialogue represents some improvement:

T: What's the theme of this term's work?
S1: Living things.
T: And how do we learn about them? David?
S2: By observation, which means looking carefully.
T: So what did we observe last time?
S3: Well, Miss, we watched things feeding off one another in the school garden . . . [she gives examples]
T: Well done, Fiona. And what are we using to try to describe what we see? Sam.
S4: Technical language – and the technical language we learned last time was 'food chain'.
T: Excellent. So, now for our next piece of technical language . . .

These students are better versed in giving answers which have some substance to them than those in the first extract. The teacher moves straight in without padding out the first sentence with unnecessary context about 'last lessons'. She has linking themes: livings things, observation, technical language. The students are aware of this. She makes a good connection between previous work and the next topic, without labouring the point and she is now ready to start work on Territory in a more positive way than the first teacher. This beginning may not be the strongest possible for the lesson – something to which we will return later in this chapter – but it is an improvement over the first example.

2 Defining the key terms or concepts

Earlier, we defined explaining. We said it was giving understanding to another person. Since understanding is at the heart of the process, it stands to reason that one cannot proceed very far unless the students share with the teacher knowledge of the meaning of the key terms or concepts being used.

In preparing explanations, one of the most important tasks the teacher has to undertake is to review the language of the explanation; and particularly the key words and phrases on which the explanation depends. This sounds simple – simplistic even. Yet many classroom problems arise specifically from failures in this area of teaching skill. Let's use Activity 9 to look at an example.

Activity 9

Understanding what is said

Read the short passage below, entitled The Blimp.

Answer the questions which appear immediately after it.

To what extent was it possible for you to carry out the task?

Did you understand what the passage was about?

If you would like to know what the passage was about, the missing information is provided at the end of the chapter.

The Blimp

Jacques sat out on the end of the garbut looking at the blimp. It was a dull day: the jinko was leaden. The blimp edged towards him; and he could feel the wind freshening on his face. The blimp was ominous: green and menacing. Its white fangs appeared and disappeared with its rolling motion, as it waited to gobble the unwary. Exposed on the garbut, with his leg damaged by the earlier fall, he knew it was only a matter of time until the blimp opened its jaws and swallowed him up.

Comprehension exercise

1 What colour was the blimp?
2 What had happened to Jacques?
3 Where was he sitting?
4 Draw and colour the jinko.

The story of the blimp has its own internal logic. If you didn't work out what a blimp, a jinko and a garbut were, you could still answer questions 1–3; and even half of question 4. You would not have been able to draw the jinko, but you could have chosen the right colour! You might have scored quite highly on the test, without actually understanding much of the story. In the same way, students may appear to be following what you say: but until you define your terms you cannot guarantee there is much shared understanding.

In the previous chapter, the teacher defined territory as 'a space, a piece of land if you like, in which an animal lives'. This was a reasonable starting point from which it was possible to build, as we shall see as we go through this chapter.

3 LINKING THE EXPLANATION WITH CONCRETE EXPERIENCE

In the course of this book it has been hinted several times that some explanations, at least, need to be based on concrete examples or real experience in order to be fully understood. It is further suggested that a reason for starting with the concrete is to heighten the impact of the explanation and to make it more interesting. How does this work in practice?

To return to the text of Territory One, all the forms of explanation that we have used so far have failed to grasp the nettle of starting with a real situation. Territory One in Chapter 3 suggested the teacher alluded to things that were happening outside the classroom window as the explanation unfolded (blackbirds singing from roofs and TV aerials). But there was no attempt to *begin* from the observed behaviour of the birds. Another way of tackling the explanation might be to have done just that: we will assume that the classroom windows look out over gardens and roof-tops, as was hinted, and that the students had been made aware of the importance of observation to scientific method. The explanation might have started like this:

T: Today's topic uses what we described as one of the scientist's most important skills: observation. Before we talk, let's look. [He moves the class to vantage points near the windows, with notebooks and pencils.] Now I want you to watch that blackbird on the TV aerial on the green roof. Record everything it does for the next five minutes or so until I tell you to stop ... make notes and sketches.

4 Using examples (positive and negative) and exceptions

Examples sometimes take the place of concrete or first-hand experience. By using examples, everyday experience and understanding can be imported into an explanation and used to illustrate what is being said. This strategy has the dual advantages of economy of time and increasing the pace of the explanation. The teacher in Chapter 3 used this method quite effectively:

Now, if you own a piece of territory, you want to mark it out as yours. When we own a house we often put up a fence or plant a hedge to mark out the boundaries. That fence or hedge borders the territory: it's a sort of signal to others that this is ours, so keep off! Some landowners put up signs: 'Private – keep out' or 'Trespassers will be prosecuted'. Birds and animals do much the same. Of course, the blackbird doesn't put up a fence, but the fence is still there: other blackbirds know it is. They know that the ground between the first bird's song-posts is already occupied.

And again, later:

Other animals use different methods to mark their territory: birds sing, but many mammals use scent. They do exactly what the blackbird does, and wander around the edges of their space; but as they go they leave traces of scent from glands, often near the tail, or they urinate, which serves the same purpose.

Quite often it is useful to give both positive examples as here, and negative examples, i.e. examples showing how something doesn't work or apply, or exceptions. In the present case the teacher could have added an exception like this:

> *But while many creatures hold territories, not all of them do. You may have seen wildlife films about tortoises in the Galapagos islands coming ashore to lay eggs: they don't hold a single piece of territory like the blackbird. They come ashore, lay, and leave. In the same way animals may urinate without marking their space: cows and sheep in the fields may do this, and that's true for other herd animals too. So, some creatures hold territories: and those that do mark them in some way.*

The purpose of using examples and exceptions is to show how the explanation works using several parallel illustrations, so that the student can draw out the concept and understand its operation by gaining a mental map of those features which are consistent from one illustration to the next and those which are not.

5 Building in tasks

It would be misleading to give the impression that an explanation necessarily happens without punctuation for other, related, learning activity. The first main area of activity which teachers may build into the explaining process is to set the students a task.

In a sense, we have already examined this phenomenon under section 3 above. There, the revised form of the explanation began with a task: to use observation skills to begin to define the area around which the explanation was to be targeted.

Tasks can punctuate an explanation at any appropriate point, besides being used to set the scene or to follow up the topic under consideration. This point is picked up again in section 15, below. Their fundamental value, though, is to involve the learners in the learning process through active participation.

6 Introducing and using technical language

Many explanations require technical language of one kind or another to be used to further the students' understanding: sometimes the explanation is of the technical language itself. No technical language can be used without the teacher being sure that all the students understand it. In Territory One, the new technical term which was introduced was 'song-post':

> *Some landowners put up signs: 'Private – keep out' or 'Trespassers will be prosecuted'. Birds and animals do much the same. Of course, the blackbird doesn't put up a fence, but the fence is still there: other blackbirds know it is. They know that the ground between the first bird's song-posts is already occupied.*

In this case the teacher *assumes* that the students will understand the term: and, indeed, the language – while used in a technical sense – is perfectly intelligible. Nevertheless, it would have been better for the teacher to have paused long enough to draw attention to the new description, to reinforce its use in a conscious way, perhaps like this:

> *They know that the ground between the first bird's song-posts is already occupied. Those points on the rooftop and the TV aerials from which the bird sings regularly are known as song-posts, for fairly obvious reasons.*

She might then have gone on and added:

> *If you plotted them on a map, and then drew lines to join one to the other, the area inside the lines would be the bird's territory.*

This may seem a small point, but in the process of 'giving understanding to another person' it can make a crucial difference.

7 Developing rules and principles

Mention has been made of how examples are often used in explanations – frequently, several of them grouped around a theme – to illustrate a point both positively and negatively. Exceptions can be used to reinforce the same learning. What emerges from this procedure is what we have called a 'mental map', for the students, of the ground being covered.

In fact, what is happening is that the consistent factors in those examples and exceptions are building into general rules or principles which underlie the understanding required of the students by the explanation. In Territory One, over the course of Chapter 3 and this chapter, we have built up a number of examples and exceptions which can aid the general principle of understanding: What is territory in the animal kingdom? These are:

> *Now, if you own a piece of territory, you want to mark it out as yours. When we own a house we often put up a fence or plant a hedge to mark out the boundaries. That fence or hedge borders the territory: it's a sort of signal to others that this is ours, so keep off!*
>
> *Some landowners put up signs: 'Private – keep out' or Trespassers will be prosecuted'. Birds and animals do much the same. Of course, the blackbird doesn't put up a fence, but the fence is still there: other blackbirds know it is.*
>
> *They know that the ground between the first bird's song-posts is already occupied. Those points on the rooftop and the TV aerials from which the bird sings regularly are known as song-posts, for fairly obvious reasons.*
>
> *If you plotted them on a map, and then drew lines to join one to the other, the area inside the lines would be the bird's territory.*
>
> *But while many creatures hold territories, not all of them do.*

> *You may have seen wildlife films about tortoises in the Galapagos islands coming ashore to lay eggs: they don't hold a single piece of territory like the blackbird. They come ashore, lay, and leave. In the same way animals may urinate without marking their space: cows and sheep in the fields may do this, and that's true for other herd animals too. So some creatures hold territories: and those that do mark them in some way.*

This mental map now has several items or rules plotted on it which build into the principle 'territory'. They are: some birds (and mammals) hold territories (though some do not); a territory is an area in which the creature lives; it is marked out; in the case of the blackbird it is marked out by singing, but there are other methods; territories can be mapped by us through observation.

While it is some way from complete, this mental map of territory-holding in the animal world is beginning to develop.

8 USING CONNECTIVES TO ENHANCE MEANING

When we speak, we often use connecting words between sentences in a quite unconscious way to enhance the meaning of what we say or to give our words a specific connotation. Consider, for example, each of the following short paragraphs:

I am going to the shops. It is my intention to buy a new dress. I shall be home again as soon as possible. The train is slow and crowded. I like to get the job done.

Sadly I am going to the shops *because* it is my intention to buy a new dress. *But* I shall be home again as soon as possible *because* the train is slow and crowded; *so therefore*, I like to get the job done.

Now I am going to the shops. *Although* it is my intention to buy a new dress, I shall *nevertheless* be home again as soon as possible. *Whenever* the train is slow and crowded, *of course* I like to get the job done.

The first example is simply a string of facts; the remaining two paragraphs alter the meaning of the first by adding connectives of various kinds. In the second paragraph one could assume the speaker was hostile to shopping; but in the third, one might guess that here was someone who generally liked shopping but might be inconvenienced on this specific occasion because, for some reason (perhaps it was pre-Christmas), the trains were likely to be less efficient than usual.

This is a fairly crude example; but the same principle applies to putting connectives into explanations: the tenor and meaning of what is said can be altered, making it clearer if the job is done well. Of course, the real trick is that it is a process which has to be done by teachers thinking on their feet as the explanation is delivered 'live'!

So let us return to the explanation in Territory One. Try Activity 10, which asks you to examine the use of connectives in a section of the explanation already quoted in other contexts.

Activity 10

Examining connectives

Read the following passage from Territory One which we are using as an example. As you read, mark all the connectives by underlining them or ringing them in red:

> ***But while many creatures hold territories, not all of them do. You may have seen wildlife films about tortoises in the Galapagos islands coming ashore to lay eggs: they don't hold a single piece of territory like the blackbird. They come ashore, lay, and leave. In the same way animals may urinate without marking their space: cows and sheep in the fields may do this, and that's true for other herd animals too. So some creatures hold territories: and those that do mark them in some way.***

Now make an assessment of the effectiveness of the use of connectives in this passage: are they well chosen? Are there omissions?

Try to improve the use of connectives here by writing your own version of the passage. You can add new connectives or change existing examples, but retain the text itself.

(NB An amended version of this passage appears later in the chapter, and you can compare your answer when you reach the appropriate point.)

9 Exploiting linguistic ploys

In the previous section we looked at the way connectives can help the continuity and progression of an explanation and put 'flesh on the bones' of it. In this section we look at a similar topic: how 'linguistic ploys' can add character and clarity to what the teacher is trying to put across.

What are linguistic ploys? It is perhaps easiest to exemplify them. Each of these would be an example:

- The first point I want to make ...
- Now this is an important point ...
- Pay special attention to this part of what I am saying ...
- I'll take these points in sequence: ...
- That's the definition, so let me tell you how it works ...
- So, now we have an understanding of how it works, we can go on to ...

So, what are linguistic ploys? They are 'signposts on the route to giving understanding'. They signpost important points reached in an explanation, the key point or points in a sentence or idea, the change of direction that is about to happen, and so on.

We can illustrate this by using the Territory One extract again. In this version, the linguistic ploys are italicised. As you read, note the difference they make to what is said:

> Now, *I am going to use a parallel example from human behaviour, so pay particular attention to this, as it may help you to understand.* If you own a piece of territory, you want to mark it out as yours. When we own a house we often put up a fence or plant a hedge to mark out the boundaries. That fence or hedge borders the territory: it's a sort of signal to others that this is ours, so keep off! Some landowners put up signs: 'Private – keep out' or 'Trespassers will be prosecuted'. Birds and animals do much the same. Of course, the blackbird doesn't put up a fence, but the fence is still there: other blackbirds know it is.
>
> They know that the ground between the first bird's song-posts is already occupied. Those points on the rooftop and the TV aerials from which the bird sings regularly are known as song-posts, for fairly obvious reasons. If you plotted them on a map, and then drew lines to join one to the other, the area inside the lines would be the bird's territory.
>
> *But I want you to realise that* while many creatures hold territories, not all of them do. *Think about this*: You may have seen wildlife films about tortoises in the Galapagos islands coming ashore to lay eggs: they don't hold a single piece of territory like the blackbird. They come ashore, lay, and leave ...

10 Using repetition and emphasis

This skill is very similar to the one described in the previous section. Just as linguistic ploys direct attention more specifically to an important point, so the teacher's repetition of something important in the explanation lends emphasis to it:

- The significant thing about this, the most significant thing is ...
- The boundaries of the territory, then, are marked by the song-posts: the song-posts are the markers.

Out of context, and written down, this may sound a little stilted. But in the real world of spoken language it will sound quite natural and spontaneous. Indeed, it is not always necessary to repeat words or phrases to give that emphasis. In the 'living voice', as opposed to writing, tone and inflection are used to do the same job. This is hard to show on the page, and can only be communicated by underlining:

But I want you to realise that while many creatures hold territories, not all of them do. Think about this: you may have seen wildlife films about tortoises in the Galapagos islands coming ashore to lay eggs: they don't hold a single piece of territory like the blackbird. They come ashore, lay, and leave ...

Repetition and vocal emphases bring the explanation to life, just as they would in conversation or story-telling in everyday life.

11 Adopting an appropriate pace

The pace at which an explanation proceeds has to be married to the speed at which the audience can assimilate what is being said. (In a sense, to judge this the teacher needs some feedback from the students: this is dealt with in section 15, below.)

In Territory One we made the point that, in the final paragraph, the pace changed: it suddenly speeded up quite noticeably, and the teacher covered a lot of points very quickly and without elaboration:

The reasons animals hold territories are several. First, if they own a space they can more easily guarantee a food supply. Then, with a nice pad to live in, the male might attract a female more easily. Once he has attracted a mate, he can breed – and if it's a good territory with plenty of food the young will probably stay alive. So, in the longer term the species will survive.

The change of pace was probably not very appropriate. If the students were new to the idea of territory, then they would have been equally new, perhaps, to the ideas in this paragraph. The teacher could have slowed the pace at this juncture, like this:

There are several reasons why animals, or birds, hold territories. First, if you have a piece of land of your own, or a few trees and so on, then you can more easily guarantee your food supply. Then, owning a territory means you have somewhere to build your shelter, burrow, nest, or whatever it is you need to live in. Once food and shelter are established, the male can think about the next important biological process: mating. So he can attract a mate to the nest knowing that, when the eggs hatch, there is a good chance the parents will find enough food to feed the young and raise them to maturity. When all these conditions are satisfied, the likelihood is that at least some of the young will themselves grow to adulthood and breed. This is the process we know by the technical term 'survival'.

While this new version of the last section of the explanation is longer, it is a good deal more explicit. Above all, it tries to make causal links between the facts as described. It is therefore a better explanation of the concept of territory – or, one might say, it better achieves the purpose of giving understanding to another person.

12 NUMBERING POINTS

This final section of Territory One teaches us another lesson: that of using 'numbered points' or verbal lists more effectively. Let us look again at the first version of what the teacher said:

> *The reasons animals hold territories are several. First, if they own a space they can more easily guarantee a food supply. Then, with a nice pad to live in, the male might attract a female more easily. Once he has attracted a mate, he can breed – and if it's a good territory with plenty of food the young will probably stay alive. So, in the longer term the species will survive.*

We noted in the previous chapter that the teacher had started to number the points as she was talking, but that the numbering faded away after 'Then, with a nice pad ...'. But suppose the teacher had not done this, but sustained the intention. How would the paragraph have looked?

> *The reasons animals hold territories are several. First, if they own a space they can more easily guarantee a food supply. Secondly, with a nice pad to live in, the male might attract a female more easily. Thirdly, once he has attracted a mate, he can breed and fourthly, if it's a good territory with plenty of food the young will probably stay alive. So, in the longer term the species will survive.*

This new version of the final section of the explanation has several merits. First, it is clearer. Second, the numbers help to focus the students' attention on each point being genuinely discrete. Finally, it begins to highlight more effectively the inter-connection between the four points which leads to the final sentence.

13 USING HUMOUR

Not all lessons are funny, nor should they be. Humour is not about telling jokes, nor is it about deviating from the topic. Often, in lessons, humour is more about a phrase which brings something to life through wit, mild amusement or pun, than it is about belly-laughs or pupils rolling in the aisles (which latter phenomena are actually distracting, not helpful). There is only one fleeting example of humour in the original text of Territory One:

> *Then, <u>with a nice pad to live in</u>, the male might attract a female more easily.*

The context of this explanation does not really demand any humour beyond this; but the fact that it is there at all alerts the reader to its value.

14 LINKING THE EXPLANATION TO OTHER KNOWLEDGE

In the life history of explanations, one of the commonest failings is to treat the knowledge that is contained within them as if it were somehow entirely discrete and separate from all other knowledge, and as if it had no links with other concepts that the students may have encountered or be about to encounter. This attitude is a significant failing of the English education system itself – but that is a debate for another book, or at least a different chapter!

The link which failed in the Territory One explanation was in relation to the concept of habitat, since students may well have heard this other word without properly drawing a distinction between the two ideas. So, at some point, specific attention needed to be drawn to the second idea (habitat), and a distinction made between it on the one hand, and territory on the other.

It is open to some debate as to the best point in the explanation for this to have taken place. It could have happened at the early, definition, stage. The definitions of both terms could have been introduced, compared, contrasted. Some teachers would have handled it like that; but I would not have done because it would have drawn away, rather than focused, the students' attention on the idea of territory.

Similarly, the habitat idea could have been left to the final paragraph. Then, with one concept firmly established, the teacher could have introduced and contrasted the second one. For my own part, I think there is a serious objection to this option, notably that the last paragraph is already preparing the ground for yet another concept: survival. To introduce the idea of habitat here would, I suspect, have confused the issue and interrupted the progression.

So I would favour putting habitat into the explanation as soon as the concept of territory has been established firmly through the use of examples, but before the idea is embellished by the four numbered points of the last paragraph about the consequences of territory-holding as a prerequisite to survival. This is what the first version of Territory One said:

> *Now, if you own a piece of territory, you want to mark it out as yours. When we own a house we often put up a fence or plant a hedge to mark out the boundaries. That fence or hedge borders the territory: it's a sort of signal to others that this is ours, so keep off! Some landowners put up signs: 'Private – keep out' or 'Trespassers will be prosecuted'. Birds and animals do much the same. Of course, the blackbird doesn't put up a fence, but the fence is still there: other blackbirds know it is. They know that the ground between the first bird's song-posts is already occupied. Other animals use different methods to mark their territory: birds sing, but many mammals use scent. They do exactly what the blackbird does, and wander around the edges of their space; but as they go they leave traces of scent from glands, often near the tail, or they urinate, which serves the same purpose.*

My view would be that the best solution is to introduce the concept of habitat as a new paragraph immediately after this one:

> *Now, we must be careful to draw a distinction between this idea of territory, and a similar one which you may have heard of: habitat. Habitat is a rather broader idea than territory. It is any area which is suitable for a creature to live in; as opposed to territory, which is a specific piece of suitable habitat which is actually occupied by a bird or mammal and of which it regards itself as the owner ...*

Having inserted this clarification into the explanation, one could then return to the main theme, probably using a linguistic ploy to signal that this was the teacher's intention.

15 Building in the feedback loop

So we come to the last skill to be considered in this chapter: the last, but by no means the last in importance.

The opening statement in Chapter 1 was that teachers talk a lot; and they do. The problem sometimes is they talk too much, or at least for too long at a stretch. An explanation can go on for quite some time, and sustaining concentration as a listener is hard – not just for students, adults would find it equally difficult. It is too easy for explanations to become monologues, or lectures, divorced from sensitivity to the needs of the audience. The way around this problem is to build in a feedback loop. This serves a dual purpose. First, it breaks up the teacher talk. Second, it enables the explainer to make some judgement about whether the explainees are understanding the subject matter.

The commonest methods of punctuating an explanation are by setting tasks and by asking questions. The first method has been mentioned in section 5 of this chapter. The second part of this book is devoted to the skills of questioning, so you can refer to this for guidance on the effective use of questions. For the moment, though, it is probably sufficient to look in summary at four important roles that questions can play in furthering an explanation as it progresses (Table 4.1).

Summary

This chapter has reviewed fifteen of the skills required of all explainers. It is not a complete and comprehensive list: indeed, as the rest of the book proceeds we shall be adding a few more skills, and some important ones have been noted in the earlier chapters, too. But what this chapter has shown is two things:

- Explaining is a complicated process, and those who want to become good at it must analyse, practise and acquire the skills involved.
- By going through these processes it is possible to improve on our explanations.

Table 4.1

Four ways of using questions to further an explanation

To establish how much students already know before the explanation starts. For example: Today's topic is about something we call by the technical term 'territory'. Does anyone know what this word means when we use it about birds or mammals?
To check on understanding during an explanation. For example: I have just used another technical term: song-post. Who can describe what a song-post is?
To provoke thought and speculation about the topic during the explanation (to avoid 'spoon-feeding'). For example: Now there is another word you may have heard which is used to mean land which a particular bird or mammal may inhabit; has anyone any idea what that word is?
To check on understanding after an explanation. For example: So let's see who can remember the definition I gave at the beginning, the definition of a territory?

So, what remains for this chapter is to revisit Territory One once more, and to see how it might look if these skills were to be built into its composition. The finished product we shall call Territory Two. Just before we do that, however, you should tackle Activity 11.

Activity 11

Revising an explanation

Look back to Territory One on pages 19–20 – you will need to photocopy the text of it and have it in front of you.

Now work through the fifteen skills reviewed in this chapter. For each skill, identify changes that would improve Territory One. (Some of them appear in the text, of course – but feel free to make your own amendments.)

Compare your revised version with the one that follows.

Territory Two

(Underlining in the text indicates use of linguistic ploys; italics indicate emphasis in the spoken word.)

T: Now you recall that we're doing some scientific *detective* work. And what's the theme of this term's work?

S1: Living things.

T: And how do we learn about them? David?

S2: By observation, which means looking carefully.

T: So what did we observe last time?

S3: Well, Miss, we watched things feeding off one another in the school garden ... [she gives examples]

T: Well done, Fiona. And what are we using to try to describe what we see? Sam.

S4: Technical language – and the technical language we learned last time was 'Food chain'.

T: Excellent. So now for our next piece of technical language. Today's topic is about something we call by the technical term 'territory'. We're going to explore what the term means, and then we'll see how it works in practice. Does anyone know what this word means when we use it about birds or mammals?

[Several suggestions, none exactly correct.]

Some of you are getting close to the idea, but let's *investigate* things a bit, and see if we can get closer. Today's topic will benefit from one of what we described as the scientist's most important skills: observation. Before we talk, let's look. [T moves the class to vantage points near the windows, with notebooks and pencils.] Now I want you to watch that blackbird on the TV aerial on the green roof. Record everything it does for the next five minutes or so until I tell you to stop . . . make notes and sketches.

[They do this: he stops them.]

Right, let's think again about what the word territory means:

Territory is a space, a piece of land if you like, in which an animal lives, and over which it has ownership.

Now, I am going to use an example from human behaviour to illustrate this idea, so pay particular attention as it may help you understand:

If you own a piece of territory, you want to mark it out as *yours.* When we own a house we often put up a fence or plant a hedge to mark out the boundaries. That fence or hedge borders the territory: it's a sort of signal to others that this is *ours,* so keep off! Some landowners put up signs: 'Private – keep out' or 'Trespassers will be prosecuted'. Birds and animals do much the same. Of course, the blackbird doesn't put up a fence, but the fence is still there: other blackbirds know it is. They know that the ground between the first bird's song-posts is already occupied: song-posts are boundary markers.

So, go back to the points you marked on your maps. The points on the roof top and the TV aerials from which the bird sings regularly are known as song-posts for fairly obvious reasons. You plotted them on your maps; if you draw lines now to join them one to another, the *area inside the lines is the bird's territory,* its territory: write the word on your map.

But you must be aware of this: Other animals use different methods to mark their territory: birds sing, but many mammals use scent. They do exactly what the blackbird does, and wander around the edges of *their* space; but as they go they leave traces of scent from glands, often near the tail, or they urinate, which serves the same purpose.

Now, we must be careful to draw a distinction between this idea of territory, and a similar one which you may have heard of.

There is another word you may have heard which is used to mean land which a particular bird or mammal may inhabit; has anyone any idea what that word is?

[They offer one or two ideas. Sam: Is it habitat?]

Good, well done: habitat. Habitat is a rather broader idea than territory. It is *any* area which is *suitable* for a creature to live in; as opposed to territory, which is a specific piece of suitable habitat which is *actually occupied* by a bird or mammal and of which it regards itself as the *owner.*

But I want you realise that, while many creatures hold territories, *not all of them do.* Think about this: *You may have seen wildlife films about tortoises in the Galapagos islands coming ashore to lay eggs: they don't hold a single piece* of territory like the blackbird. They come ashore, lay, and *leave* ... In the same way animals may urinate without marking their space: cows and sheep in the fields may do this, and that's true for other herd animals too. So, some creatures hold territories: and those that do mark them in some way.

But let's move on to the next important point.

There are several *reasons* why animals, or birds, hold territories. First, if you have a piece of land of your own, or a few trees and so on, then you can more easily guarantee your food supply. Second, owning a nice pad to live in – a territory – means you have somewhere to build your shelter, burrow, nest, or whatever it is you need to live in. Third, once food and shelter are established, the male can think about the next important biological process: mating. So he can attract a mate to the nest knowing that, when the eggs hatch, there is a good chance the parents will find enough food to feed the young and raise them to maturity. Fourth, *when all these conditions are satisfied,* the likelihood is that at least some of the young will themselves grow to adulthood and breed. This is the process we know by the technical term *'survival'.*

Now that's rather a lot to take in. So let's see who can remember the definition I gave at the beginning, the definition of a territory? Then I am going to ask you to write up some of what we have learned ... Jake, do you remember the definition? ...

(In the passage The Blimp, the following real words were replaced by nonsense words: pier – garbut; sea – blimp; sky – jinko.)

Outcomes

At the end of this chapter you should have:

- Understood the fifteen skills for explainers and how they work in practice, individually and together, to enhance an explanation
- Empathised with pupils who find explanations difficult
- Specifically, examined the role of connectives in making explanations 'work'
- Practised improving your own explanations in the light of these skills.

FURTHER EXPLAINING SKILLS

5

OBJECTIVES

This chapter invites you:

- To consider the different audiences for explanations
- To look at ways of using explanations to raise pupils' thinking levels
- To use a range of resources to make explanations more compelling
- To be aware of some common errors in explaining.

So far in this book you have examined and analysed into types some sample explanations in technology, in history and in science. From these you have been able to identify the basic explaining skill: sequencing. You have also been able to deduce fifteen further skills which all explainers need. In this chapter you will look at a further group of explaining skills, before moving on in Chapter 6 to consider the wider role of explaining in a whole school language policy.

In everything that you have learned so far the assumption has been made that the preparation and delivery of your explanations will be to a group or groups of students whom you know well. For this reason the need to tailor the explanation to the level of ability of the audience has not been stressed. But now is the time to look more rigorously at this.

1 TAKING ACCOUNT OF THE AUDIENCE

All the skills which have been dealt with so far can be used to prepare an explanation for any group of explainees: they are generic skills. The same principles would apply whether the explanation was to be given to a Key Stage 1 class or in the form of a lecture to PhD students. Of course, the content, the pitch of the language, the length of time spent talking and so on, would each vary – the explainer would make professional judgements about these individual topics. But the principles would hold firm. However, it is important to pause at this point and to note that explanations need to be tailored for individual audiences.

At one level this might appear a simple thing to do: in a school with streamed classes, the pitch or level of the explanation is likely to be higher for the A band than for the D band. But most classes, even streamed classes it could be argued, do not actually contain students of precisely similar abilities: every class is a mixed ability class. In practice, some are more mixed than others, and in many primary schools the range can be quite dramatic.

Provision for abilities within the class, then, has to be a consideration early on in the planning process for explaining: it cannot be left to chance. In practice, an explanation has to include a basic core of material which is intelligible to everyone in the class, and some material which will capture the minds of, and stimulate, the most able.

This differentiation happens in part through the words the explainer uses; but it will also operate in the questions they ask during the explanation, and through the tasks set to the students which relate to the topic being explained. One form of differentiation, through raising the cognitive stakes in explanations, is dealt with in the next section. (You should also consult the companion volume in this series: *Learning Objectives, Task Setting and Differentiation*.)

2 RAISING THE COGNITIVE STAKES OF EXPLANATIONS

It has been suggested that one of the measures of effective teaching is the amount and depth of thinking which students are stimulated to do: their cognitive activity. If we think of an explanation for a moment divorced from any associated questions or tasks – in other words we concentrate purely on the 'teacher talk' element of it – then how can this be used to stimulate improved cognition in students?

Research, discussed in Chapter 8, investigated teachers' questions and discovered that, while teachers are talking they are giving out signals, through their words, of the cognitive levels at which they want students to operate.

This research collected hundreds of samples of 'teacher talk' of various kinds, e.g. questions, explanations and instructions, and analysed them for cognitive demand on students, using a very simple coding system, thus:

- **Data** – the lowest level, it consists of the transmission of factual information without comment or embellishment, for example, 'Henry the Eighth had six wives'; 'Full stops are used to show the end of a sentence'; 'One-quarter add another quarter makes one-half'.
- **Concepts** – a higher level, which consists of considering reasons, explanations and causes, for example, 'The solemn feeling in this poem is helped by the metre'; 'Graphs are useful because they allow us to gain a visual image of a set of figures'; 'The shape of this valley is the result of the action of ice during the last Ice Age'.
- **Abstract ideas or generalisations** – the highest level, which consists of rules and principles, for example, 'So the scientist must conclude from the evidence that this phenomenon has a genetic cause'; 'This leads to the formula $A = \pi r^2$'; 'Something can be good without being just . . .'

The outcomes from this research indicated that the explanations which were most effective at stimulating students' thinking were the ones where the teacher was able to move from data into the two higher orders of cognition. So how does this work in practice?

Activity 12

Analysing the cognitive demand in explanations

Read the transcript below called Block Graphs.

Use coloured pens or highlighters (three colours) to identify those sections of the explanation which are at the Data level, the Conceptual level and the Abstract level.

Tape-record an explanation of your own from one of your lessons; make a transcript and carry out the same exercise on that. Summarise what you have learned from these two exercises.

Block Graphs

Yesterday I split you into groups of six. In your group you took it in turns to measure the length of the footprint of other people in the group: so you have now got six measurements, each one in centimetres. I told you that today we were going to discover a new way of putting this information down on paper.

Right, now I have given each of you a large sheet of paper which is printed out in centimetre squares. At the bottom of the sheet we are each going to draw a straight line like this, 6 cm long [demonstrates on squared blackboard].

Good – all done? Right, at the left-hand end of that line we are going to draw a line going up – what do we call that? [Jo: Vertical.] Yes – so before we draw it we need to know how long it's going to be. Who had the largest feet in the class? [They compare.] Jason – and his were 27 cm long, so we'll draw that line 27 cm high. Do that.

So, now we have a kind of L-shape, 27 cm high and 6 cm along the base. Let's number the squares going up, as far as 27 – the left-hand corner where the lines join is zero, then the first printed line is 1 and so on up to 27 at the top. [They number, the teacher checks.]

OK. Next we are going to make a column to show Jason's foot. We're going to make it how high? [Steven: 27.] Correct, but 27 whats? [Tracey: Centimetres.] Good, 27 cm. And how wide? [Pause, while they think. Nick: We could do it 1 cm wide.). OK, let's try it. Let's colour in a column 27 cm high, and 1 cm wide. [They do.] But how will we know that's Jason's foot? [Toni: We could put his name on the bottom by his square.] Good. Do that now.

Let's take the next square along. Steven, you gave a good answer just now, we'll put your measurement on next. What was it? [Steven: 19 cm, Miss.] So, let's add another column, 19 cm high: use a different colour this time – and don't forget to put Steven's name at the bottom, because this column represents Steven's foot.

Now, in a few minutes you are going to make a block graph like this of the feet of the people in your group of six, using the other side of this sheet of squared paper. Before that, I want to do two more things. First, let's recap what we've done. We've drawn an L shape. The line along the bottom – the horizontal line – has 1 cm length on it for each person in the group; so if there are six in the group it is 6 cm long. How long would it be if there were eight in the group, Tanya? [Tanya: 8, Miss.] Eight what? [Tanya: 8 cm, Miss.] Right each centimetre along the bottom line represents one person in the group. And the vertical line – this one – has to have 1 cm for each centimetre of the longest foot in the group. This vertical line represents the length of the foot. You remember we started with the longest measurement in the class, but in your group that largest number may be smaller than 27. So, that leads me to the second thing I want to tell you.

The second thing is this: I want you to put the measurements on your graph in size order starting with the largest and ending with the smallest. The way to do that is to write down your six names and measurements on these six little pieces of paper I am giving your groups now, then put the papers in a line on your table with the largest first and so on. Then transfer the measurements in order to the graph. OK – everyone understand?

[They carry out the task.]

Everyone stop now. Most of you have finished; those who haven't can finish in 'Quiet Time'. Before the lesson ends I want to just go back to putting your numbers in order. You put them on pieces of paper, largest first, then down to the smallest. We call that Rank Order. So if I said to you: Rank order these numbers [writes 5, 7, 3 on the board] – what's the answer? [Tommy: 7, 5, 3, Miss.] Good – biggest first, then down to the smallest, each one smaller than the previous one and bigger than the next. Next time I'll see who can remember what rank ordering is!

In Activity 12 and the explanation 'Block Graphs' you will have seen how the teacher moves from data level operation, which makes little cognitive demand, into higher levels of thinking. At the end of the lesson the performance of these young students is getting quite sophisticated.

They proceed through the data level (revising, drawing a line), to the conceptual level (putting sizes in order), to the abstract (the meaning of the horizontal and vertical axes).

3 SUSTAINING FLUENCY AND DEFEATING MANNERISMS

The intellectual success of an explanation depends on raising the cognitive stakes, as we have just seen. By contrast, the accessibility of an explanation to its audience depends on characteristics such as interest, pace, and fluency. Some of these have been dealt with in the previous chapter. Here it is opportune to consider how, as explainers, we can maintain and improve fluency.

Obviously, explanations in which the explainer is familiar with the subject matter and is well prepared are likely to be more fluent than others. However, the key to many failures of fluency is often in the words chosen by the explainer and whether they slip into the kinds of habits which, while they are almost unnoticeable in colloquial speech, become serious irritants in sustained explanations.

Taking the explanation at a steady pace, and thinking on one's feet about the choice of words and connectives, will help an explanation to flow. But what often intrude are those nasty habits of speech like y'know, OK?, actually, at this moment in time, the point is is that, and so on – phrases we all use but whose pointlessness is aggravated by repetition. One otherwise superb commentator on Test Match cricket always used to begin his analysis of a batsman's shot with the words: 'Really speaking ...' By the end of five days this habit could develop a state bordering on neurosis in the listener!

There is a simple remedy for verbal mannerisms: tape-record your lessons from time to time and play them over, listening for the tell-tale signs.

4 Using audio-visual stimuli

In a previous chapter it was suggested that explanations can be improved significantly by a judicious use of examples. At that stage it was decided not to interrupt the flow of the argument or digress to discuss one specific way of exemplifying issues in the classroom: the use of audiovisual aids.

Visual aids in particular are of paramount importance in teaching. They serve as concrete experience for students on which they can build mental images, and hence understanding.

Table 5.1

Using audio-visual materials to aid explaining

Some kinds of audio-visual materials helpful to explanations:

- overhead projector transparencies – self-made, or commercially produced: there are even some which provide 'working models' for technological subjects
- slides, photographs, wall-charts, interactive white boards
- pictures culled from journals, magazines, etc. (sustain quality of presentation by good mounting of materials, for example)
- video and audio tapes
- CD-ROMs and computer programs
- photocopied worksheets (sustain quality of presentation: check items are clear and are word-processed accurately and without spelling errors, typos, etc.)
- working models, mock-ups, etc.

Some purposes to which audio-visual materials can be put to aid explaining:

- To replace or augment examples
- To add realism
- To provide concrete or second-hand experience
- To reinforce a point made orally
- To add interest and promote curiosity
- To break up a long explanation with something more tangible

Of course, audio-visual stimuli come in a variety of forms – see Table 5.1 for just a limited range of examples. The explainer's task is to consider, at the preparation stage, what kinds of audio-visual stimuli would be helpful and to find or create these ready for use at any appropriate moment in the explanation. The old saying has at least a grain of truth in it: one picture is worth a thousand words.

AVOIDING THE COMMONEST ERRORS IN EXPLAINING

Finally in this chapter, we can look at the remaining most common errors in explaining and, through awareness, begin to avoid them.

Having spoken about the positive skill of sequencing explanations correctly, it is almost inevitable that a common error in poor explanations should turn out to be the omission of one of the items in the sequence of key points that make up your explanation. For example, this would be a crucial omission:

Firing a rifle

To fire this loaded rifle safely, at a given target, is fairly straightforward. First, you check that the safety catch is on. Second, raise the rifle to the shoulder as I have demonstrated. Third, line the U of the rear-sight up into the leaf of the front sight, which is in turn in line with the centre of the target. You now have all three items lined up. Fourth, hold your breath (to stop the rifle moving) and squeeze – don't jerk – the trigger to first pressure. Fifth, (when you're rock steady) move the trigger to second pressure, which fires the gun.

Quite a careful, brief, explanation – what a shame the charging rogue rhino just gored the hapless hunter to a horrible death! All because the instructor forgot to say when to remove the safety catch.

So, omissions can make all the difference in whether an explanation is effective or not; and the same basic insight would apply to explaining, in the correct order, the sequence of items comprising the explanation.

In the example above, had the hunter taken the safety catch off before the rifle went to the shoulder, he could have blown himself or one of his companions to the promised land.

Another common error is to allow nerves to take over the explaining process, and to give in to the temptation to rush. Practice and confidence will cure this fault.

Other ways in which it is possible to run into trouble, with students not understanding the explanation, are: to leave out the feedback loop and to fail to give opportunities for the students to ask questions on what is being explained. A good habit to get into is to make regular – though not too frequent – pauses for the listeners to interject legitimately. (This is specially valuable with adult audiences, who often are too polite to interrupt to indicate that they don't follow the explanation.)

Another skill for effective explainers is summarising. Summaries can be either:

- terminal, i.e. they occur at the end of an explanation and pull together the *key* points, or
- intermediate, i.e. they occur from time to time within an explanation, pulling together the learning so far before the explainer makes a *new* point.

Finally, the most fatal error of all is failing to understand the topic which you are trying to explain. If *you* can't understand it, no one else will: that's guaranteed. So, at the preparation stage, make absolutely sure of what you are trying to communicate to your potential audience. If you can't understand the topic, work on it until you can. Remember, if you found it hard, your students will too; so find a simpler way of putting the ideas across than the way in which they were put across to you. Fall back on audio-visual aids, examples and verbal images to help. In Chapters 1 to 5 we have covered the key skills which an explainer needs. Chapter 6 examines explaining in a broader context.

Outcomes

At the end of this chapter you should have:

- Recognised a variety of audiences for your explanations and how to adapt to them
- Practised analysing explanations for cognitive demand
- Transferred the learning about cognitive levels into your own explanations
- Begun to avoid the commonest errors in explaining.

---

6 EXPLAINING AS PART OF A WHOLE LANGUAGE POLICY

OBJECTIVES

This chapter invites you:

- To explore the skill of explaining as part of a whole school language policy
- To examine explaining from the pupil's point of view
- To relate explanations to the pupils' skills of oracy.

In this book an attempt has been made to look at the skills of the effective explainer and to see how these can have a positive effect on learning. But there are real dangers in concentrating on explaining. These are encapsulated in a quotation from Peter Woods:

> *So much pupil learning in schools is alienated in that it consists of other people's knowledge purveyed in transmissional mode.*
>
> (*Contemporary Issues in Teaching* (1996). London: Routledge, p. 127)

This is a view which has to be taken seriously, and not least because a good deal of political 'wisdom' on educational issues has recently stressed the formal approach to teaching. This assumes that when teachers are teaching, students are learning. There is plenty of evidence that contradicts the inevitability of this connection.

Such a construction of the teaching process is inadequate, though it has a simplistic appeal. The facts are that:

- one aspect of the teacher's role is to give effective explanations;
- some of the student's commitment is to listen to them;
- the more effectively explanations are constructed, the more learning will occur; and
- teachers' explaining skills can be improved using the techniques identified and described in this book.

However – and it is a very significant 'however' – explaining cannot, and should not, be divorced from its wider contexts.

Explaining is one, and only one, of the weapons in the armoury of the teacher and occupies only part of the teacher's time. Explanations have to be given a grounding in the whole bedrock of classroom language activity, too. In this chapter we will go on to examine how explanations can be seen as part of a 'whole language' policy for the school, and we examine what that means for the teacher.

At the heart of the issue is an examination of the kinds of language activities that go on in every classroom. These are very varied and certainly include the following:

- teacher talk, including explanations
- teacher questions
- student questions, responses and listening
- students' writing
- teacher–student discussion
- students' exposure to experience – both first- and second-hand
- the affective domain, i.e. conversation
- language performance, for example, drama
- reading, silently and aloud
- group interaction
- presentation to peers.

This is a modest list of classroom language activities, but it will serve for the present purpose. Let us examine each of these categories of language in turn.

TEACHER TALK

This book has been dealing with the 'formal' business of giving explanations. But explanations of this kind do not exhaust the kinds of verbal transactions which take place in classrooms and which are teacher-led. For example, one would hope that a whole ethos in classroom activity is built on social exchanges between teachers and students. In the school in which I work, students start arriving at about 8.30 a.m. for a 9 a.m. start. They spend the time in a variety of ways: catching up on, or getting ahead with, set work; using the computers; looking at magazines; accessing the library for projects or for interest, and so on. A good deal of student–teacher interaction goes on at this time. Much of it is organisational, some of it relates to learning, and part is simply what – outside school – would pass for conversation.

The importance of the language itself, and the incidental learning that goes on in this time, should not be underestimated. Much can be conveyed which influences attitudes, and has spin-offs into discipline and behaviour. The talk and language at this time is a significant factor in building school ethos. Informal language may be just as important as formal language – such as explanations – in determining what happens in school and how much students learn. As far as I am aware, no one has researched this well enough to say. This element of teacher talk does not fit comfortably into the 'political model' quoted earlier – but no sane teacher would be without it. It is certainly important enough to be included in the language policy of the school in recognition of the role it plays in the life of the school.

TEACHER QUESTIONS

Part Two of this book covers questioning skills, so we will not go into detail here about the role of questions in learning. Suffice it to say that we have already noted how explanations are inevitably punctuated by teacher questions. We will see that, just as explaining can be improved by an analytical understanding of the skills associated with it, questioning can be too. Teacher questions are so crucial that they have to have a place in language policy – a place which guarantees that they will be used in a planned way to enhance explanations, to provide feedback, to challenge, and to raise the cognitive stakes in lessons, for example.

Students' questions, responses and listening

Part of the cut-and-thrust of teacher explanation is the important act of students participating through feedback and interaction with the material they are studying. Students have a role in classroom talk, and that role is significant. The proposition of this book is: students have not learned until they have articulated for themselves the material to which they are being exposed. Learning is not passive listening, it is not even mindless regurgitation. It involves a sophisticated range of abilities:

- to understand the topic
- to reformulate material
- to use it
- to analyse it
- to re-structure it
- to question it
- to weigh evidence from it
- to reject those parts of it that don't stand scrutiny.

These are rigorous intellectual processes. They may not be politically attractive as part of a theory of education, because such intellectual skills may be directed who knows where? But these are crucial factors in genuine intellectual development, and it is never too soon to begin students on the path to acquiring these skills. School language policies should articulate them as part of their learning intentions.

The same holds true for listening. Students are required to listen for many hours every day. Intelligent teachers understand that concentration for even the most dedicated has its limitations. While students' listening and concentration skills can be systematically enhanced through exercises and practice, many teachers know that it is better to set aside times for close listening. Such times can relate to periods of explanation, and be flagged up as of special importance. This does not relieve the student of the obligation to listen at other times, but signals what we all know – that we listen with varying degrees of attentiveness at different times. Listening times can be punctuated in a planned way by other activities, such as reading or writing, or practical tasks.

Students' writing

Much school language is written language. Though students are asked to write in many different styles and for a variety of potential audiences, they are most frequently asked to reproduce knowledge in written form, or to investigate issues in writing. These classroom tasks involve explanation. Just as the teacher needs explaining skills in front of the class, so the students need those same skills to respond to written tasks. For this reason, explaining skills for students need to be included as part of the learning intentions of a school's wider language policy.

TEACHER–STUDENT DISCUSSION

The topic of discussion as a teaching method is discussed in Chapter 16. There it will be argued that formal discussion (as opposed to conversation) is a valuable learning tool. This may be in the form of a debate, or in the less restricted format of opinion-giving at the teacher's invitation. By whatever rules discussion functions at a particular classroom moment, one of the key skills needed by the participants is the ability to articulate their views logically and clearly – in other words to explain. Again, explanation features at the heart of the language activity of the school.

STUDENT EXPOSURE TO EXPERIENCE

Part of becoming articulate, and of explaining things clearly, is to have experiences on which to base one's knowledge. In the skill of explaining some emphasis has been placed on second-hand experience: the use of examples, and of visual aids. Much of what takes place in school can, and should, be based on either second- or first-hand experience. By second-hand experience I mean things that can be accessed from books, from video and so on: the student cannot experience old age directly, for example, but can gain some experience of it from observation, or from accounts of and by old people. First-hand experience means those things that can be assimilated immediately, through the senses perhaps, such as carrying out a scientific experiment and smelling the resulting gases. Plowden (1967) pointed out the value of concrete experience for younger students, but there is hardly an adult among us who doesn't learn more enjoyably and more effectively through direct or indirect experience: this insight explains the move by many museums to interactive displays. This immediacy in learning improves the ability to know, to empathise, to reflect, to draw conclusions and ultimately, therefore, to articulate.

THE AFFECTIVE DOMAIN: CONVERSATION

Conversation – in this case between students, since teacher–student conversation has been dealt with already in this chapter – is not explaining: but the same skills are important. A good conversation requires the account to be ordered appropriately, for there to be choice of language (such as connectives) that enhances the telling, for there to be pauses for comment, questions and feedback from the second person

– all features of explaining. Conversation is a forerunner of more formally constructed language. The early morning time in my school, described above, and break times, are ideal opportunities for students to engage in social talk which itself is valuable as a learning medium. In a more formal secondary school in which I was once employed, there was no such opportunity early in the day. So I used to break with convention and invite students to talk with each other before registration for a few minutes. There were rules, of course, which kept noise low, but I felt the practice improved both learning and all-round social relations.

Language performance: drama

Though drama is a different discipline from explaining, drama and explaining have mutual spin-offs. In drama one has to perform to an audience, which is true also of explanations. In explaining, the impact is sometimes aided by a little acting!

Reading and reading aloud

A lot of reading matter is explanation. When a passage is read aloud, the explanation has to be assimilated quickly by the reader, so that expression can be imparted to it. Private reading requires students to access information: and requires the writer to have explaining skills. Once more we see how explaining interacts with other language areas which are part of a school's whole language policy.

Group interaction and presentation to peers

These two areas can be taken together because similar activities are involved. Teachers often set tasks to be tackled in learning groups. The dynamics of the learning group are such that members have to share knowledge and assist each other to learn: explaining is an integral part of that process. More formally, representatives of these learning groups may be asked to present their findings to their peers. This is a common classroom activity which depends directly on the explaining skills of the student carrying out the presentation. The student as teacher needs the same skills as those of the teacher.

Summary

A whole language approach in school has the following features that mark out its quality:

- It is cross-curricular – all subjects are involved in delivering its intentions.
- It is conscious – it forms part of the declared intentions of the school for its students.
- It is planned – teachers devise deliberate activities which further its achievement.

- It is progressive – students' skills are built up over time.
- It is practised – teachers take every opportunity to reinforce the skills.

In this brief review of the possible content of whole language policy, links have been made between the other elements of it and the skills required of teachers and students specifically as explainers. These skills, it is suggested, are integral to language across the curriculum and should be practised consciously on every appropriate occasion. Given this assertion, perhaps it is opportune for you to review your own school's policy and your own classroom practice in this area.

Activity 13

Reviewing whole language policy in the context of explaining

Obtain a copy of your school's whole language policy.

Analyse the policy in the light of the material in this chapter.

Is the role of explaining – by teachers and by students – adequately represented in this policy?

What could be improved? How?

What steps could you take to bring these improvements about in the school and in your own lessons?

Some thoughts about oracy

As long ago as the Bullock Report (1975) there has been a recognition that students learn more effectively when they articulate what they have learned:

> *... every teacher in every school should accept it as part of his [sic] responsibility to develop the pupils'... speaking ability in and through the subject or activity for which he is responsible ...*
>
> (Bullock Report, para 237)

In our discussion of questioning, the point is made (in Chapter 12) that this skill is not a teacher-dominated domain: students can ask questions too. So with explaining, students should be encouraged to emulate the teacher in engaging in productive classroom talk – which will include explaining and the skills that go with it.

Oracy is the other side of the coin to teacher talk: the moment when the roles are reversed and the student emulates the teacher. This is how one writer construed it:

> *Children learn by talking and listening, and should be given more opportunity to talk. Children talking in small groups are taking an active part in all their work. Tentative and inexplicit talk in small groups is the bridge from partial understanding to confident meaningful statement. Present talking is future thinking.*
>
> (Sutton, C. (1981) *Communicating in the Classroom*. London: Hodder & Stoughton)

Whole books have been written about oracy. Some of the most pertinent information comes in the Norfolk Oracy Project (1992) report (NOP), compiled by Ann Shreeve. NOP points out that teachers need to audit the talk that goes on in their classrooms, and suggests a useful framework against which this can be done. The framework consists of four sub-sections and an adapted version is included as Table 6.1.

Table 6.1

Auditing students' talk

1 Talk to what purpose?
- To explore or solve problems.
- To argue a case.
- To explore an issue.
- To narrate a story or event.
- To persuade others.
- To instruct peers.
- To evaluate.
- To summarise.

2 By what means?
- Through joint planning.
- In a working party/task group.
- In discussion.
- With/without notes.
- In a structured debate.
- Through anecdote.

3 To what audience?
- To peers.
- To a large/small group.
- To an unknown group.
- To adults.

4 Using what techniques?
- Presentation.
- With or without questions to/from the audience.
- Body language.
- With or without visual aids.
- Brief or extended period of time.

Tarleton (1988) points out, rightly, that:

> *We cannot expect children to improve in oracy without making explicit the skills behind the words ... (p. 49)*

So he makes a case for teaching students, quite explicitly, explaining and talking skills of the kind on which this book is based, and of the kind implicit in Table 6.1. He emphasises that students have to realise that talking is a way of learning. They have to know that what they say will vary according to: the audience; the purpose of the talk; and the style of the talk (for example, discussion, formal debate, and so on). He lays particular stress on teaching voice control, body language, and the ability to form a relationship with the listeners. All these are useful points.

Too often, teachers do not realise, and certainly do not plan for, the many kinds of classroom talk which can occur – most of which rely on explaining skills for their success. The range is shown in Table 6.2.

Table 6.2

Examining the range of classroom talk

Students may engage in any of the following kinds of classroom talk:

- explaining to peers
- giving information to peers or adults
- arguing a case
- defending a point of view
- analysing a situation or problem
- offering suggestions and ideas
- asking questions
- answering questions
- contributing to peer discussion
- debating – in a formal setting
- giving a speech (for example, of thanks, to a visitor)
- negotiating a solution to a problem
- hypothesising
- narrating an event or story
- describing
- giving instructions to a peer
- challenging the opinions of others
- evaluating ideas or materials
- weighing evidence
- offering conclusions
- summarising

POSTSCRIPT

Some teachers may have found this chapter a little off-putting. For while the whole book asks the reader to stand back and examine their teaching skills and techniques, to subject something as basic as talk to analytical scrutiny can be a bit daunting. In this context, some words of Cazden (1988) may be comforting. After completing a long and learned volume which analysed classroom discourse, he wrote:

> *Finally, a word from one teacher to others. Thinking about the research reported in this book will inevitably lead to greater self-consciousness, at least temporarily. It did for me, and I wish this didn't have to happen ... But as anthropologist Edward Sapir explains, 'It is sometimes necessary to become conscious of the forms of social behaviour in order to bring about a more serviceable adaptation to changed conditions ... analysis and conscious control are the medicine of society not its food.' (p. 199)*

Outcomes

At the end of this chapter you should have:

- Located explaining and explanations in your total language behaviour and policy
- Developed an empathy with pupils' reactions to explanations
- Audited the range of student talk in your classes and used the findings to mould your behaviour.

7 Explaining in other contexts

OBJECTIVES

This chapter invites you:

- To examine giving instructions as a form of explaining
- To scrutinise the skill of giving written explanations
- To relate explanations to composing materials through the medium of ICT.

So far, we have explored the skills which a teacher needs in order to become an effective explainer; and we have noted that students themselves need explaining skills in order to function effectively as learners. In this chapter we will look at three particular, rather specialist, aspects of explaining. The first of these relates to giving instructions; the second to written explanations; and the third to the links between explaining and the new technologies.

Instructions as explanations

Classroom life is packed with instructions. Many of these are quite brief: Sit down, Be quiet, Get out your books, Use pen not pencil. But our concern is with longer sets of instructions to students – the kind of instructions which set up classroom tasks and activities.

These instructions are, in fact, explanations in disguise. They are almost always What? explanations: This is what I want you to do. They may include elements of How? and of Why? In other words, they set parameters for how the task is to be tackled and they explain the purpose or desired outcomes of the task. Here is a typical example:

Devising a role play

Right look this way. So, we have all now shared this reading about Simon.

Simon was an old man trying to cross the road – but he was frail and slow; and panic set in when the lights changed as he was half-way across. When I tell you, you are going to move into the working groups we identified earlier, and carry out a task – a very important task.

Pay close attention to what I want you to do: You are going to imagine that you are Simon, and you are going to act out a scene like the one from the reading.

First, your group has got to discuss what will be included in the scene, and how it is to be portrayed. Then you have to allot the various parts to members of the group. Thirdly, you must rough out and rehearse your playlet, ready to perform it. Fourthly, each group will get a chance to perform to an audience from another class. However, before you start, listen carefully to what we need to get from this exercise. This is what you have to think about in your groups: The audience must feel the tension which Simon felt. So you have to create that tension; and later you will be asked to explain how you did this.

Finally, you need to know why we are doing this. It's because I am going to make an assessment of each person's oral skills. So you will need to speak clearly, loudly enough to be heard by the audience, and choose your words sensibly.

You may now move into groups.

This explanation is, in reality, a set of task instructions. Sometimes these are given orally, as here; sometimes teachers write such instructions down. For example, a set of written instructions may be used for a homework task or to guide a classroom test.

The penalty for getting instructions wrong is that students' efficiency at carrying out the task becomes impaired. This can lead to chaos and indiscipline in extreme circumstances – but it is not such an uncommon occurrence for new teachers. Before you read on, carry out Activity 14.

Activity 14

Analysing a set of instructions

Go back over the instructions above: 'Devising a role play'.

Use the template of explaining skills provided in Chapters 4 and 5 to assess the effectiveness of the instructions.

What could have been improved?

Now find some written instructions that you have provided for one or more of your classes recently. Carry out the same exercise on these. How effective were they? How could you have improved your own performance at giving instructions?

WRITTEN EXPLANATIONS

Chapters 1 to 5 dealt with the skills of explaining orally in class; and the section above transferred those skills to oral instructions. In addition, the point was made there that instructions can be written as well as oral. So it is with all explanations: indeed, perhaps the majority of explanations in post-school life come in written form – how to fill in your tax return, what is happening to the euro, why candidates think we should vote for them, how to get the most out of your computer – and many other examples. In school, many explanations are written down. Perera describes the problem in these words:

> *I am interested in the fact that many children who can read simple stories competently and with enjoyment have great difficulty in understanding their school textbooks. Teachers of pupils in the 9 to 14 age-range often complain that they cannot find textbooks simple enough for children to read independently. Comprehension problems may arise from either conceptual or linguistic complexity . . .*
>
> (Perera, K. 'Some linguistic difficulties in school textbooks' in Gillham, B. (ed.) 1986)

In this context, if one were to recap on the explaining skills listed in Chapters 4 and 5, one would find they all applied to written explanations in some degree. There would, of course, be some variations. Obviously, written explanation cannot rely on voice control or intonation to add emphasis, for example. But the skill is simply transferred into the use that is made of verbal ploys: emphasis, repetition, and the use of connectives become more significant. Punctuation takes over some of the role of spoken emphasis.

Table 7.1

The skills of written explanation

Skill	Written explanation
1 Identifying types of explanation	Relevant
2 Sequencing	Fundamental
3 Thinking of a dynamic introduction	The reader's attention has still to be captured
4 Defining the key terms, concepts	Relevant
5 Linking with concrete experience	Can be achieved on the page by diagrams, tables, graphs, photos, as well as through reference to putative student experience
6 Using examples	Equally applicable
7 Building in tasks	Can be achieved through interactive texts – like this one
8 Introducing technical language	Equally applicable: use of glossaries can be helpful
9 Developing rules and principles	Equally important – text can be used to highlight these – see the next section of this chapter
10 Using connectives	Even more important the written word has to do the job of the teacher's emphasis
11 Exploiting linguistic ploys	As 10
12 Using repetition	Equally important; thought can be given to repeating ideas in different words
13 Pace	Texts have two 'paces' – the pace at which the ideas flow in the teacher's writing, and the pace at which the learner reads. 'Skim readers' are an explainer's nightmare as they may miss crucial stages in the sequence.
14 Numbering points	Much easier in text and the use of bullet points, different typefaces, etc., can distinguish the parts of an explanation and add variety, interest
15 Using humour	Equally valuable
16 Linking to other knowledge	Equally valuable
17 Feedback	Can be achieved in an interactive text, but is otherwise a missing stage over which the explainer has no control
18 Taking account of the audience	The explainer has to do this whenever the audience is known – sometimes in written explanations the target audience is out of sight and out of one's control
19 Raising the cognitive stakes	Equally important: all teaching embraces this ideal
20 Sustaining fluency, removing mannerisms	Written explanations are less likely to suffer from fluency problems; verbal mannerisms are easier to see and control on a page
21 Using visual stimuli	The written page lends itself to the inclusion of some forms of visual stimuli – see 5 above
22 Avoiding errors	A written explanation allows more time and opportunity for review by the explainer

Table 7.1 reviews the skills of oral explaining, identifying how they apply to written explanations.

So written and oral explanations share many features, but some qualities of a good explanation have to be adapted to fit the medium. Something written explanations have which oral explanations do not have, in visible form, is punctuation. You might like to consider the role of these kinds of punctuation marks in written explanations:

- the exclamation mark
- the question mark
- the bracket
- the colon
- the quotation mark.

To explore this topic, try Activity 15.

Activity 15

Practising a written explanation

Think back over your recent teaching, when you gave explanations to a class. Pick one explanation.

Put this explanation down in writing – draft it first, review it, refine it until you are happy with it.

Go back over your written explanation and try to work into it (relevantly) as many of the six forms of punctuation mentioned above as you can. Do they help?

Judge your written explanation against the 22 criteria listed in this section.

EXPLANATIONS AND THE NEW TECHNOLOGIES

This series of books on teaching skills aims to examine traditional skills that are still relevant to the teacher, and to explore new skills which must be acquired. It also scrutinises the traditional skills to see how they need to be adapted to emerging situations. In the field of explaining – a traditional skill – the adaptation must be primarily to the new technology of computer use in schools.

One of the emergent trends of the early years of the twenty-first century is inevitably going to be to give students more control over their own learning. All kinds of factors contribute to this trend: the move by some schools to a five-term year or other forms of year-round education (already common in the USA); the universality of computers in all aspects of non-school life; the decreasing costs of this technology; the move to home-based working, and possibly home-based schooling. The simple hypothesis is this: increasingly in the next two decades students will work 'home-based' or 'resource-centre based' in their learning. Which means: they will need materials to work with. The teacher's role will shift from the didactic, in front of groups of students, to the dual roles of:

- mentoring students in resource centres, who will be carrying out private study, and
- generating the materials the students use for that study, either on-screen or as printouts.

If this hypothesis proves to be even partially accurate, then far from abandoning the traditional skill of explaining, teachers will need to become even more proficient at it in order to produce computer-based learning materials. Some of these may have wider applications than use with their 'own' classes – and may be subject to more open scrutiny than are oral classroom explanations now. So this is a skill worth refining!

This book has set down all the skills that a teacher will need in order to explain effectively using either oral or written media, including those for writing the instructions for how to proceed with a piece of (computer-based) work. However, it is worth pausing over a related set of skills which will enhance this kind of teaching: the layout and design of computer-based explanations.

In producing work on computer, some of the following attributes of the finished product may support and enhance the explaining process:

- identifying and sustaining a house style
- keeping page layout simple
- choosing an appropriate, clear typeface for the main text
- manipulating typefaces effectively for emphasis and clarity
- having a clear, consistent system for main and sub-headings
- using numbers, bullet points, etc., appropriately
- using space intelligently to add emphasis
- avoiding the pitfall of confusion due, for example, to the overuse of artwork
- using tables, diagrams, etc., to clarify points
- use or non-use of colour, shading, etc.

Clarke (1997), albeit he was working with Higher Education students, found that the order of popularity of illustrative material in computer texts was:

- realistic illustrations
- cartoons
- line drawings
- diagrams
- charts and tables
- analogies.

He also found the optimum size for such graphics was one-quarter to one-half of the screen; that overuse of colour to gain attention became counter-productive; and that users like sequential routes through computer-based materials.

One advantage of studying on a computer rather than using printout is that the student can interact with the computer program. The program has the potential to allow for the feedback loop: a student's knowledge can be checked, and if it is deficient he or she can be back-tracked until they have mastered that stage of the explanation or content.

One of the biggest differences between explanations in computer-based learning and oral classroom explanations is the period of time over which the explaining has to be sustained. In generating written resource materials the teacher has to sustain the explanations over a considerable quantity of text. This calls for much thought to be given to the language used, and to the way in which ideas are built up through the text in order to achieve improved cognition. In fact, one could do worse than bear in mind Gibbs' (1992) definition of a quality learning experience:

> *... the development of students' intellectual and imaginative powers; their understanding and judgement; their problem-solving skills; their ability to communicate; their ability to see relationships within what they have learned and to perceive their field of study in a broader perspective ... to stimulate an enquiring, analytical and creative approach, encouraging independent judgement and critical self-awareness.*

It should be borne in mind that some students will much prefer this style of working to traditional teaching; others will be less fluent in the technology and less content with the lack of social contact which is implicit in it. Both audiences have to be satisfied. Some teachers, too, will have doubts. Many of these are based on the view that technology dehumanises. While one may have some sympathy with that view, it is important to listen to the voices of those who do not agree. For example, Jagodzinski *et al.* (1997) actually claim:

> *Multimedia has the potential to return us to a more sympathetic culture in which many aspects of learning are recognised as requiring first-hand, or at least simulated, experiences of the real world. (p. 213)*

That is precisely the position of this text of explaining skills: that good explanations plug into the students' own experiences or, failing that, help to provide them.

Outcomes

At the end of this chapter you should have:

- Through analysis, understood the nature of instructions as explanations
- Practised written explanations
- Considered the role and nature of explanations in ICT-based learning.

REFERENCES ON EXPLAINING NOT OTHERWISE CITED IN THE TEXT

Bell, C., Bowden, M. and Trott, A. (1997) *Implementing Flexible Learning.* London: Kogan Page.

Bourne, J. (1994) *Thinking Through Primary Practice.* London: Routledge.

Brown, G. and Hatton, N. (1982) *Explanations and Explaining.* Basingstoke: Macmillan.

Cazden, C. (1988) *Classroom Discourse.* Portsmouth NH: Heinemann.

Clarke, A. (1997) 'Screen design of computer-based learning materials' in Bell *et al., op. cit.*

Gibbs, G. (1992) *Improving the Quality of Student Learning.* London: Technical & Education Services.

Gillham, B. (ed.) (1986) *The Language of School Subjects.* London: Heinemann.

Jagodzinski, P., Phillips, M., Rogers, T. and Smith, C. (1997) 'Models of knowledge, learning and representation for multi-media learning environments' in Bell *et al., op. cit.*

NOP (1992) *Oracy.* Norwich: Norfolk Oracy Project.

Plowden Report (1967) *Children and their Primary Schools.* London: HMSO.

Sutton, C. (1981) *Communicating in the Classroom.* London: Hodder & Stoughton.

Tarleton, R. (1988) *Learning and Talking.* London: Routledge.

Wragg, E. and Brown, G. (1993) *Explaining.* London: Routledge.

PART TWO

QUESTIONING

8

Why do we need questioning skills?

OBJECTIVES

This chapter invites you:

- To consider the nature and purpose of questioning in the classroom
- To relate the technique of questioning to your overall philosophy of educating
- To begin to reflect on the relationship of questioning to theories of learning
- To discover some facts about classroom questioning as revealed by research.

Enquiry lies at the heart of the education process; and enquiry takes place through the formulation of questions, problems and hypotheses which require answers and solutions.

The purpose of this book is to examine the place of questioning in the classroom: to identify precisely why questions need to be a key part of the teacher's armoury; to discover that questions differ in their nature and effectiveness; and to learn some of the skills involved in asking better questions and asking them more effectively.

This book is essentially a manual of practice – it is aimed at things teachers can do in classrooms to improve their skills of questioning, It will ask you questions, and request that you interact with the text by carrying out a number of Activities designed to reveal or improve your practice in questioning. But the practice and processes of teaching must be built upon a sound framework of research and theory. The best teachers always have an underlying framework to their teaching that acknowledges their personal synthesis of why one should teach in a particular way. Conversely, atheoretical teaching is always flawed because it cannot answer the crucial 'Why?' questions about the job. For this reason, this chapter deals with some theoretical considerations and some of the research which underpins questioning. It is perfectly possible for you to skip this chapter and still make sense of Part Two – but if you do this, we hope you will return to it when you have tried out some of the ideas and found that they work. This chapter may help to explain why!

Theoretical considerations

The Draft Handbook makes both explicit and implicit references to questioning. Implicitly it demands high standards from pupils and asks the teacher to challenge youngsters – both processes well served through questioning (para 3.1.1). Similarly, the Handbook requires teachers to provide strategies that make demands across all ability groupings – something it is almost impossible to do effectively without using questioning as a key tool (para 3.1.3). Again, on a social level (para 3.2.1) questions are used to make contact with pupils' interests and concerns.

Explicitly, in para 3.2.1, the Draft Handbook requires use of 'a repertoire of questioning techniques, which are inclusive and which encourage pupils to contribute, to expand on topics, to reflect, to evaluate, and to share relevant personal insights and experiences.' In the same way, sections on communication and language (e.g. para 3.2.2) imply a high degree of questioning. Indeed, I would argue that one cannot promote the five thinking skills of para 3.2.1 (information processing, reasoning, enquiry, creative thinking and evaluation) without recourse to frequent questions by the teacher and from pupils to the teacher and each other. Para 3.2.5 specifically links questioning with discussion – and a short chapter is devoted to this topic later in the manual. Even in the requirement to assess pupils' work effectively during lessons (para 3.3.1) there is an implication that some of this will be done orally, i.e. through questioning leading to feedback; and para 3.3.2 requires teachers to 'identify pupils' misconceptions and other difficulties in the course of teaching' – an outcome, in the main, of questioning. Questioning by pupils of their own work as a form of evaluation appears in para 3.3.3, while an acknowledgement that teachers can use 'different styles of questioning' appears in para 3.4.7.

If there is a criticism of any of these approaches it is merely that too often the context is pathological, i.e. it is about putting things right rather than getting things right in the first place. This manual aims to put questioning at the very centre of the teaching process and acknowledges its absolute centrality to every teacher's skills base.

The fact that the Draft Handbook has such clear, explicit and important advice on questioning makes it doubly unfortunate that the current national standards for teachers, encapsulated in QTT (TTA 2002), make virtually no reference to this skill.

Activity 16

Identifying your philosophies

Try to set down in a paragraph or so your personal philosophy of education and the theoretical framework which characterises your teaching methods. Bullet-points rather than continuous prose will suffice.

Now think about the questions you ask in your own lessons, and set down some information about them, for example:

- What kinds of questions do you ask?
- When do you ask them?
- Of whom?

- For what purpose?
- When you choose to teach using questions, why do you select this method rather than another?

Check your outcomes with what follows in this chapter, noting any similarities and differences.

(It may be helpful if you keep the written responses to all your Activities in a file so that you can refer back to them later to see how your practice has changed and developed.)

The history of questioning is lost in the mists of time. Some hundreds of years BC in ancient Israel, Job was asking ultimate questions about suffering, life and the purpose of the universe. Across the Mediterranean, Socrates built a lifetime's reputation on his ability to ask challenging questions – questions so challenging that he paid the ultimate price. That is something worth remembering because, while teaching through questions is unlikely to cost you the same fate, it is a more adventurous way than the seemingly interminable teacher talk which appears to have found political favour recently. Perhaps the difference between didactic talk and teacher questions is a simple but profound one: the former assumes we teachers know the answer to the problem under review, while the latter leaves open the possibility that we may not.

But if questioning is spiced with a pinch of the unknown and a hint of unpredictability, that makes it potentially all the more effective. Provided, that is, that one's philosophy of education values such things. Three decades ago one might have termed such an approach 'child-centred'. This phrase has fallen into disrepute at the present: it is supposed to smack of a looseness of thinking epitomised by the Plowden Report (1967) into primary teaching. In fact, anyone who has read the text of Plowden knows that it was saying – three decades ahead of its time – much the same as what many educators believe today about good practice in teaching. It asked teachers to begin from where the child is: a process which all good teachers espouse every day in both primary and secondary schools. This book, therefore, assumes that what goes on in the classroom is built upon the needs of the student, and that the questions teachers ask are designed to promote learning from that point.

How does learning occur? There are numerous theories, some of them immensely complicated. Here, we will sift out the bones of some of the most relevant for the present context.

Behaviourist models

While some theories may be valuable for underpinning some kinds of learning, they may be less helpful in explaining the value of asking questions. For example, most people are familiar with the Behaviourist models – they had their genesis in Pavlov's experiments with animals: a dog trained to come to its food by the sound of a bell, would salivate to the sound even when lunch was not provided! This kind of thinking was developed into classroom-based theories by Skinner and Thorndike, and these emphasise the role of 'drills' (such as saying tables or reciting French verbs), value practice ('Do two hundred more of the same kind of sums'), and point to the importance of reinforcement ('Read this poem again for homework').

Behaviourism has its problems as a theory in the context of learning through questioning. It does not place much value on starting from where the student is and using existing knowledge. It is low on teacher interaction with students; and it ignores the range of abilities which occur in most classes. It is a way of teaching that has value for certain activities that are suitable for reduction to rote learning, but must often be inadequate as a way of furthering learning and stretching intellect.

Constructivist theories

More helpfully, Constructivist theories suggest that students learn through an interaction between thought and experience. This is a valuable step forward since it takes us into the realm of child-centredness. But the variation called Social Constructivism is more productive still. Social Constructivists tell us not only that we must begin from the student, but that the social interactions of learning (between teacher and student, and between student and student) are also significant. This theory underpins collaborative classroom working, group-based activities, discussion methods by teachers and so on. The teachers with their questions become the agents for challenging groups and taking their thinking on, having first ascertained by the same means what students already know and understand.

Social Constructivist theories depend on a view which places language at the heart of the learning process. In this context we must mention the work of Lev Vygotsky. This Russian psychologist held that talk was not about the transmission of facts, its significance was in the communication between the developing child and others with more knowledge. Through talk the developing child moved towards the development of intellect and the higher cognitive processes. This view has implications not only for the role of the teacher, but also for the significance of collaborative, i.e. social, learning.

An extension to his theory is the concept of the 'zone of proximal development' (ZPD). Effectively, this theory says that students learn incrementally: beginning from what they know they 'scaffold' knowledge on to this base to build a structure of understanding. Questions in the classroom, then, may provide the rungs on these ladders of understanding.

These Social Constructivist theories, along with Vygotsky's work on language and the ZPD, provide us with a basic theory of learning which supports the use of classroom questions. But there is still the matter of the student's developing intellect to consider in a little more detail. In what has been written above, care has been taken to link knowledge with understanding. Much of the early debate about the National Curriculum centred on what students should know rather than on what they should understand. Indeed, it could be argued that undue emphasis on knowledge at the expense of understanding is – in educational terms – the 'English disease'. We are far too concerned with the acquisition of data for its own sake, and too little concerned to manipulate that data to learn something useful from it. In the same way the English are obsessed with 'subjects' and 'subject expertise', and frequently miss the vital connections between subjects that lead to real insight.

Piaget's developmental theory

To deal with this problem we need a theory of learning which addresses these issues. The best-known learning theory is probably the developmental theory of Jean Piaget. This identified developmental stages in children – sensori-motor, pre-conceptual, intuitive, concrete operational, formal operational – and this theory is useful because it suggests that, as a general rule, the intellectual abilities of students progress with age. But, inevitably, such a theory can be only a rough guide: and there is plenty of evidence to suggest that, while all children progress through these recognisable stages, some do so at a breathtaking pace, and others much more slowly than the norm. The teacher must not make the facile connection: age eight years = concrete operations; rather, he/she must look at the student and ask 'What stage on the model has this child reached?' This takes us back to our preferred child-centredness approach, but in a context of intellectual growth.

Bloom's work on thinking skills

However, to be really effective we need not only to know the stage a student has reached in intellectual terms, but to understand how to define and categorise the student's thinking skills. Such an attempt exists in the work of Benjamin Bloom. Bloom talked about high and low order thinking skills. He was able to distinguish between those operations which required a minimal level of intellectual activity to achieve, and those which provoked depth of thought and understanding. In this context, 'rewarding' a student who has just got ten sums right with the task of carrying out another twenty almost identical calculations would engage the student in lower order thinking (practice, reinforcement). But to ask the student to take the learned skill and apply it to a new situation ('You have found the area of some of these rectangles; using squared paper can you find how to work out the area of this circle?') would be to require higher order thinking (in this case, application). Teachers' questions are thus capable of provoking either low or higher order thinking in students.

Metacognition

The intellectual or cognitive effort which is required of students in our schools needs to be directed purposefully; and the work of Jerome Bruner can help us here. Bruner believed that authentic learning took place not when the learner was given pre-extant solutions, but when they were presented with 'real life' problem-solving. A feature of this approach is its emphasis on the need to cross subject boundaries: solving real problems frequently requires skills from a variety of disciplines. Bruner believed that learning was supported, too, when the learner reflected on their own learning processes – what he called metacognition. Such ideas were developed by Bruner, but were not new: they have their origins in, for example, the discovery methods advocated by the American John Dewey early in the twentieth century. They fit well into the philosophy of questioning as a teaching/learning tool advocated in this book. They uphold the student-centredness principle, support the key role of language and social learning in classrooms, and suggest that challenge and problem-solving are the routes to improving intellectual performance.

RESEARCH FINDINGS

So now we have some theories, what about the research?

Before describing some relevant research it is perhaps appropriate to set down some hypotheses and questions.

What has been said in this chapter so far suggests that research into questioning needs to explore matters such as:

- To what extent is questioning used in class as a teaching method?
- How is it used?
- Do teachers ask intellectually demanding questions of pupils?
- Could the proportion of intellectually demanding questions asked in classrooms be usefully increased?

Before exploring these one might hypothesise that:

- teachers ask a lot of questions;
- a small proportion of questions asked in classrooms make high levels of cognitive demand on students;
- increasing the cognitive quality of questions is a matter of learning to be self-analytical and then working on improved techniques.

So what do researchers research when they look at teachers' questioning behaviours, and what have they found out about teachers' questioning patterns and skills?

Classifying questions

The first problem which researchers encounter is how to classify questions in order to study them. A relatively common answer is to divide them simply into two categories:

OPEN ________________ CLOSED

An open question permits a range of responses, but a closed question implies that the teacher has a predetermined 'correct' response in mind. The description 'pseudo-question' is used to refer to a question which appears open but in practice requires a closed answer or action; for example 'Would you like to sit down quietly now?' usually means 'Sit down and stop making a noise!'

Another classification might be:

RECALL ________________ THOUGHT

Here, the choice is between pre-existent knowledge by the pupil, and the need for the pupil to pursue the topic further on their own behalf.

There are more complicated ways of classifying questions, and since we are concerned with cognitive demand we need to consider at least one example. In some of my research I adapted the classification of Benjamin Bloom to divide questions into the following kinds:

0	Management questions	Low order
1	Recall	
2	Simple comprehension (i.e. where the answer has previously been provided)	
3	Application questions	Higher order
4	Analytical questions	
5	Questions requiring synthesis	
6	Evaluation questions	

Brown and Edmondson used a similar system which drew both on Bloom's work, and on what teachers told them about the kinds of questions they asked. They were right to suggest that all classification systems are potentially flawed – and real insight into questioning needs to take on board contextual factors which are too subtle for the classification systems to handle. Nevertheless, such systems do give us some basic insights into what goes on when teachers ask questions. Table 8.1 on page 73 gives typical examples of question types 0–6.

Activity 17

Trying out some analysis of your own questions

At this point you may find it helpful both in understanding the process of question analysis and in starting to think about your own questioning skills, to undertake some systematic scrutiny of your own lessons.

Tape-record a half-hour segment of a lesson when you think you will be using questioning as a tool to aid student learning. Take the tape home, play it over slowly, and write down each question you asked.

Go through your list of questions and score each one on the categories 'open' and 'closed'.

Go back through the list of questions and score each one again. This time use the categories 'recall' and 'thought' questions.

Finally, go over the questions a third time and try to decide about each whether it falls into Bloom's low order or higher order categories (just mark them 'L' and 'H' for now).

You have now analysed the same questions in three different ways. Review how you got on by scoring the results on this grid:

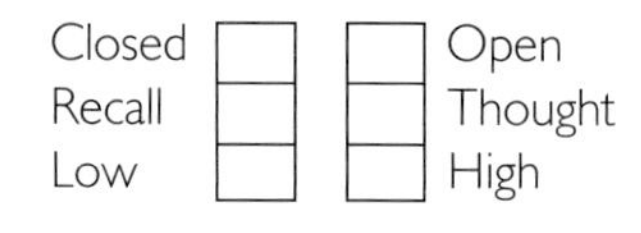

Now that we have examined and practised with some research tools, the time has come to discover what research reveals about classroom questioning. However, since a theme of this book is that it is desirable to encourage students to take 'intuitive leaps' towards solutions to problems, try Activity 18 before you read on.

Activity 18

Speculating about questioning research

Using your experience as a teacher and knowledge of classroom practice, try to answer each of the following questions. When you have attempted all of them, read on to discover what research has revealed.

1. What percentage of teachers' questions do you think is concerned with the recall of facts?
2. What percentage of questions do you think is concerned with the management of classes?
3. What percentage of questions do you think demands higher order cognitive skills from students (i.e. those which fall into Bloom's categories 3–6 inclusive)?
4. Do you think primary or secondary teachers ask a larger proportion of higher order questions of their students?
5. How many questions do you think the average teacher asks in a professional lifetime (40 years)?
6. Do you think mathematics teachers or modern linguists ask the greater number of questions per lesson on average?
7. Is higher order questioning in class a factor in helping students do well in exams?
8. Do teachers question in the same way lesson after lesson (i.e. is their question technique based on habit)?
9. What do a teacher's questions reveal about that individual?
10. Has the advent of the National Curriculum had an impact on the kinds of questions teachers ask? If so, what kind of impact?

What research has revealed

Now that you have taken some intuitive leaps, and attempted to 'best guess' the researchers' findings, we can look at what they found. The percentage of questions of any given type tends to vary from one classroom study to another, as one might expect. What all the major research is agreed about is: the highest-scoring category of classroom question is 'recall' – a low order operation. The percentage may vary

Table 8.1

Examples of low and higher order questions

Low order

0 Management questions:
Would you run this errand for me?
Will you stack those chairs up, please?

1 Recall questions:
What did we say a noun was?
In our experiment, what happened to the copper?

2 Comprehension questions:
Where did the boy in the story we've just read run away to?
Which of these three colours I am showing you is the darkest?

Higher order

3 Application questions:
Given the information you have just learned, how do you think you could devise a better experiment?
How might someone make this journey in a shorter time?

4 Analysis questions:
Why do you think that schools will be different in 20 years' time compared with now?
What evidence might we look for to support this theory?

5 Synthesis questions:
How could you apply this theory of levers we learned in physics to understanding the importance of the ancient Egyptians as architects?
In understanding the history of Spartacus's slave rebellion, what do we need to know about the geography of Italy?

6 Evaluation questions:
What factors made you warm to the central character in this book?
What moral dilemmas were faced by the king?

from about 60 per cent upwards. You may be surprised to know that management questions (or, sometimes, pseudo-questions of the 'Would you sit down, please?' variety) make up between 12 and 30 per cent of all teachers' questions. In my own research into secondary schools (KS3) only 3.6 per cent of all teacher questions fell into one of Bloom's higher order categories. Interestingly, though, Wragg found that, in primary schools, this figure was approaching 10 per cent. In some follow-up work I found that in KS4 examination groups the proportion of higher order questions might actually drop; but some primary teachers reached levels as high as 44 per cent of higher order questions.

The number of questions which teachers ask – and therefore the professional effort and significance which this teaching skill assumes – is staggering. It has been calculated that, since most teachers ask an average of 43.6 questions per teaching hour, in an average career they are likely to ask between 1.5 and 2 million questions! In secondary schools, teachers of mathematics ask around this number of questions, typically; but modern linguists, at an hourly rate of 76, could expect to ask somewhere between 3 and 3.5 million. So, on that evidence, getting questioning skills honed seems an effective thing to do.

However, the value of higher order questions may have less to do with passing examinations, and more to do with developing students' cognitive and critical faculties. A number of researchers have suggested that higher order questioning in class does not have a measurable effect on students' abilities simply to pass examinations. Indeed, the evidence that higher order questioning falls off in examination groups (above), suggests that passing examinations requires more repetitive and conformist skills of students.

There is certainly evidence to suggest that teachers use the same repertoire of questioning skills, and the same patterns of questioning, lesson after lesson. The number and type of questions used by an individual teacher tends to remain constant from one observed occasion to another. Like driving a car, bad habits picked up early in one's experience tend to become permanent; which is why learning to question more effectively is so important.

Just as this text began with a statement about the theoretical underpinning on which it is based – its philosophy – so teachers' questions could be seen to signal the individual's view of education. Teacher questions reveal what kind of thinking that person expects from students; and sets the whole tone of learning in that class: enquiry, conformity, regurgitation, speculation and so on.

Outcomes

At the end of this chapter you should have:

- Understood more about the questioning process from a research point of view
- Begun to integrate questioning into your overall approach to teaching skills
- Learned how to analyse questions into 'types'
- Scrutinised your own practice as a questioner.

Why ask questions?

9

OBJECTIVES

This chapter invites you:

- To consider nine answers to the question: Why ask questions?
- To identify, from the answers, nine rules for effective questioning in classrooms
- To meet the demand of the National Standards by using questions to challenge pupils.

Reasons for asking questions

In Chapter 8 we began to look at the theories of learning which support the need to use questions in our teaching. In this chapter the focus shifts to the more practical business of asking questions in class. Yet we still need to go on asking: Why? What are the pragmatic reasons for asking questions as a weapon in the teaching armoury? Here there will be an attempt to flesh out answers to this question: in fact, nine answers (as subheadings in bold type). There will also be an attempt to generate some of the resulting principles on which lessons can be built (these are set in boxes). So, why ask questions?

1 So that pupils talk – and talk constructively and on-task

Joyce Grenfell used to do wonderful monologues of classroom life which were full of exhortations to imaginary children to sit quietly and listen to the teacher. Not much has changed! Be a fly on the wall in any classroom where 'pupils are energetically expressing their individuality', as one educator put it, and you will hear those same exhortations to silence and attention to the teacher.

Questioning transfers the emphasis in learning from the teacher to the student. The teacher enquires, probes, challenges; the student is required to think, speculate, contribute.

The first hurdle which has to be crossed by the would-be classroom questioner is to establish a culture of learning in which students expect to be actively involved and to make positive contributions. This goes against the frequent expectations of classroom life.

However, such contributions have to be disciplined. The teacher must – and it is a process that takes a little time and some practice – establish the ground rules of the new learning ethos. Students must, for example:

- learn not just to rush in with unconsidered remarks
- stop to think before answering
- listen to the contributions of others, not interrupt
- accept there may be many points of view or alternative solutions offered.

These skills have to be taught and learned in the early days of using classroom questions systematically.

One of the most common phenomena in introducing students to learning substantially through questions is to discourage them from making distracting, humorous or irrelevant remarks. Their answers have to be targeted to the topic concerned. There is nothing wrong with humour, provided it is genuinely directed to the question: but irrelevance simply destroys the learning process.

Establish the ground-rules right from the beginning.

Activity 19

Establishing the ground-rules

Select a class; then choose a lesson, or a segment of a lesson, which you think can be appropriately taught using a question-based approach. Prepare the lesson carefully around the key questions.

Before the lesson, explain your ground-rules to the class, and the reasons for them.

Teach the lesson. (You may think it is worth taping the lesson, because it makes later analysis easier to handle.) Pause whenever necessary to remind students about the ground-rules. Afterwards, you might reflect on how well the students were able to keep to the ground-rules, and decide whether any of them need amendment in the light of experience.

Assess how effective the lesson was. (You could try asking the students for their perceptions.)

2 To signal an interest in students' thoughts and feelings

One of the easiest ways in which to proceed towards the use of questioning as a learning technique in class is for the teacher to establish a pattern of conversation with students outside lesson time. Conversation is the main method by which human beings carry out normal social intercourse, an everyday phenomenon which we all recognise and value. Teachers who make themselves available for conversation with students, about anything and everything, have already prepared the ground for learning through questioning.

In some primary schools students may arrive at school quite early and be allowed into the classroom before the bell. This non-lesson time is an opportunity for them to share their news and their interests, and it gives the teacher a chance to talk informally: to engage in conversation. In a secondary school similar opportunities may arise through out-of-school clubs and activity groups. Form tutor periods can be used in this way sometimes; and even playground duty can have its opportunities for conversation. One measure of a successful teacher is whether youngsters want to talk to them. Note the way in which students have often learned to stay aloof from regular members of staff, and yet flock around a student teacher and in a very real sense enjoy their company.

Students will not open up and engage in classroom dialogue unless they feel that they can talk freely and in a conversational manner: i.e. that their thoughts are valued and of interest.

Create an appropriate learning ethos.

3 To stimulate interest and awaken curiosity

Learning through questioning has, as one of its attractions, the fact that students can be challenged – and therefore, hopefully, made interested in the learning. If I have a criticism of teaching in general it is that work is often not made sufficiently interesting for students. One of the worst primary lessons which I observed was a geography lesson about the upland areas of Britain. There were photocopied maps for everyone, with features marked but not named. On this warm, wet afternoon, with the condensation running down tightly shut windows and the humid air inducing drowsiness in the post-lunch trough of concentration, the teacher spent 90 minutes with a blackboard getting Y5 students to write in the names of ranges of hills at her dictation. As labelling the Quantocks and the Mendips gave way to labelling the Pennines and the Cairngorms, everyone except the teacher was probably yearning for a video-clip of the character of these romantically-named places, places foreign to the students' experience; and they would probably have been more motivated by tales of Roman legionaries on the Pennine forts, of climbers lost in the fog-bound snows of Exmoor with the rescue helicopters grounded, or of dotterels – smart little birds found on the very pinnacle of the Cairngorms. These students lived in the fens of Eastern England, and many of them hadn't been outside their village; it is no exaggeration to say that some would not have seen a hill, and could have no concept of the sheer magic of a sunset over Coniston or a storm on Snowdon, nor even the pastoral tranquillity of sheep roaming the South Downs in summer.

The problem here is that, as educators, we are supposed to be expert communicators, but others often do that job better – and students know that! They watch the television soap operas: Neighbours, Coronation Street, Eastenders and Home and Away. They know that every episode ends with a crisis, an unsolved mystery, an ambiguity. Yet, for most teachers, their instinct is to tidy up the ends of lessons, to dot the 'i's and cross the 't's, to give the final answers. But the trick is to make the students want to come back next time for the answers – or to pursue the questions further – not to go away sated, as if what they had learned was all that there was to know.

Keep the students curious.

Activity 20

Stimulating curiosity

Select one lesson a day for a week. Make sure that, at the end of each selected lesson, you finish with an unsolved puzzle, or a question for students to think about before next time. Make the selected problem interesting. (It is best **not** to set the question as a formal task, for example, for homework.)

Record the questions you have set, and remember to return to them at the start of the next session with the class (or next day, perhaps, in the primary sector).

Did the students follow up your question or puzzle?

How effectively?

If not, try to ascertain why not.

Did some talk about the topic to you, or each other, outside class?

Continue to use the method and see how it develops – but not for every lesson, otherwise it loses its freshness.

4 To encourage a problem-solving approach to thinking

Students whose attitudes are characterised by curiosity need a problem-based approach to learning. When we use questioning as a key teaching skill we move out of the realm in which amassing huge amounts of factual and data-based knowledge becomes an end in itself, and move into that in which it becomes the manipulation of that data and the use made of the facts to further understanding which predominate.

This is an important philosophical divide. Some teachers argue that the compulsion to 'cover' National Curriculum inevitably means that there is not time for an investigative approach in the classroom. This book challenges that view. Indeed, in the secondary sector before the National Curriculum, teachers used to claim the same about the five years of secondary curriculum in the run-up to the GCSE, and before that about the GCE O levels. It wasn't true then, and it isn't true now! Syllabuses are neutral: they describe what has to be covered, not how the learning is packaged.

In Chapter 8 we saw that investigative approaches to learning in both sectors have a good pedigree, and fit coherently into the theory of learning adopted in this manual.

Make investigation central to your teaching.

5 To help students externalise and verbalise knowledge

Asking questions puts the onus of learning where it belongs: on the student. Students have to put their ideas, speculations, thoughts, feelings and hypotheses into words. This process is in accord with the Social Constructivist theories described in Chapter 8. The value of sharing knowledge in a group was described there; but here I want to concentrate more on the value to the individual of putting learning into words. If we take a caricatured teaching situation we might describe it thus:

> *The students sit in rows and listen. The teacher stands at the front and talks. This talk contains information, possibly some explanation. The teacher dictates notes by way of reinforcement. At the end of the lesson all the students take away identical notebooks.*

I have seen this lesson in primary, secondary, further and higher education institutions throughout the land. The contention is that the students are not sharers in this process, they are spectators at it. They don't manipulate the information, they record it. They don't absorb the explanations, they reproduce them. They don't necessarily understand the subject matter, they regurgitate it. The knowledge is not theirs, it remains the teacher's.

Much of what passes for learning in our schools and colleges is of this ilk. Questioning is one way in which we can break the chain of this repetitive process.

In learning through questioning, students have to go through a number of processes which reinforce and extend real learning. These include:

- feeding back to the teacher their present state of knowledge
- having to meet the challenges of the material
- having to think aloud, with all its attendant dangers, in a collaborative situation
- having to open up their minds to alternative solutions
- having to make choices
- having to find appropriate language in which to express ideas
- having actively to use technical language and terms.

This kind of learning is shared with the teacher but does not 'belong' to him or her, nor can it be 'implanted' in someone else's brain en bloc. Some student teachers set up a video camera and went into the corridor to accost passers-by. They said: 'You are on camera. You have 60 seconds. What is education?' One passing colleague replied: 'I am an expert on Joseph Conrad. Education is to give English students my knowledge.' That is precisely what questioning claims not to do.

Make students own the problem.

6 To encourage thinking aloud and the intuitive leap

Several times in the course of this book there has been reference to the need for students to hypothesise or make intuitive leaps (guesses, even) in response to the challenge of problem-solving. This is an essential skill for those who are encouraged to learn through questions and problems – a skill rather undervalued in more didactic contexts. For this reason there may be some initial resistance to it from students. They have been schooled, in many cases, into offering only safe – that is, correct – solutions under all circumstances.

Inevitably, to pursue this kind of classroom procedure implies trust between the teacher and the students. Teachers have to guard their behaviour so that they do not make negative or disparaging remarks to students who offer incorrect or even misguided notions. The teacher's skill when this happens is to back-track and approach the issue afresh with a new line of questioning.

The intuitive leap may include what is sometimes called creative thinking or lateral thinking – but the labels are not synonymous. Given a problem such as 'How can we improve traffic flow around our neighbourhood?' a student may offer creative solutions (for example, build a covered escalator around the village so that people can step on and off anywhere, and they will leave their cars at home), or solutions involving lateral thinking (e.g. instead of people moving to services – the shops, Post Office, doctor – the services could come to them to reduce traffic flow). But intuitive thinking may simply reach a solution or set up a hypothesis without having to articulate all the intermediate steps: for example, a student might offer the idea 'We could re-phase the traffic lights to cope better with the majority of the traffic flow.'

However one labels the ideas which flow from the students, one of the essential missions of learning through questioning is to open up a channel of ideas in the classroom.

Encourage the intuitive leap.

7 To help students learn from, and respect one another

Much emphasis has been placed on what Bloom labelled the 'affective domain', that is the social interaction between teacher and students, and between student and student. The point will not be further laboured here except to say that it is important to recognise that the teacher is not always the fount of all knowledge. Students need to be helped towards understanding this truth – and the truth that, however clever, they will never become such a source of all-knowing either! Many of life's problems are better served by collective insight where each member of the group brings his or her own special emphases or insights.

Value everyone's contribution.

8 To monitor the extent and deficiencies of student learning

An important aspect of questioning in classrooms, and one of its commonest uses, is as feedback to the teacher. Through initial questioning in a lesson, a teacher can quickly establish what students have assimilated from previous sessions; and further questioning during a lesson will give an indication of gains made. The value of this kind of questioning as a teaching tool has been noted in the predominance of recall questions in lessons, as revealed through some of the research reported above. We have also noted that this kind of questioning on its own is not adequate to fulfil the potential of questioning as a teaching tool.

Monitor the learning in progress.

9 To deepen thinking levels and improve conceptualisation

As we have seen, one of the declared aims of effective questioning is to lead students from low order to higher order thinking. From the teacher's point of view, this requires planning at the lesson preparation stage with regard to the sequence of questions that will be asked about the topic studied. In asking questions the teacher will need to be making constant assessment of the 'cognitive level' at which dialogue in the classroom is proceeding. The commonest procedure is for teachers to begin at relatively low levels of thought – recall, data – and to try to progress towards more demanding thought by asking for explanation, reasoning and evaluation from pupils to support the answers they are giving or the contributions they are making to the lesson. The following short piece of classroom dialogue captures the essence of this approach:

T: Who can remember what we were talking about at the end of the last lesson?
P1: Colour.
T: Yes, but not just colour – what was the other important word?
P2: Camouflage.
T: Exactly – so who can define camouflage?
P3: It's using colour to hide something.
T: Good. Now we are going to think today about ways in which animals use colour to hide. Can you think of some examples?
P4: Some black and white animals come out at night.
T: So, how exactly does their colour camouflage them?
P4: It's like light and shade – in the moonlight.
T: Right ... [students produce more ideas ...]
T: Now the point of this camouflage is what?
P5: So they don't get eaten.
T: OK – what words might sum up that idea?
P6: Salvation?

P7: Safety?
T: Not bad ideas – but there's a specific word that scientists use. It also begins with 's' . . .
P2: Survival.
T: Great. So what concept have we just worked out here – we're scientists and we have just made a discovery . . . what is it?
P5: Camouflage colouring is for survival.
T: That's exactly right, Well done!

This example starts quite simply and moves relatively quickly to higher order thinking. But sometimes it may be judged appropriate to begin with a challenge that demands that students start to think immediately within the higher orders. This ploy is quite a good one for encouraging debate; for example, after a prominent news item about racial violence the previous evening, a teacher might begin a PSE lesson by asking the class 'How do you think racism can be challenged in this school?'

In the business of teaching through questions, the progression to higher order thinking is the constant goal towards which the teacher must strive.

Raise the cognitive stakes.

Activity 21

Asking challenging questions

This Activity asks you to try your hand at challenging students. Select two or three lessons in the week where you are likely to be covering material in which there is some element of controversy or debate. Plan, for each session, a challenging question to act as a lead into it.

(An example might be as follows. The teacher is working on the theme of health and the topic of smoking. A challenging question could be: 'Since smoking is hazardous to smokers and non-smokers alike, should we tax smoking out of existence in order forcibly to improve people's health?' Or if the theme was World War II and the topic about the everyday life of people in London, a question might be: 'Would you have made evacuation of children compulsory?')

In your notes, record:

- the theme and topic
- the challenge you set
- the reaction to the challenge
- how successful a range of ideas it produced.

(Remember, controversial areas can sometimes cause pain or offence, so select your questions carefully, phrase them as sensitively as possible, and leave scope for a range of responses.)

Outcomes

At the end of this chapter you should have:

- Begun to empathise with the ten rules for effective classroom questioning
- Practised one of the rules: on establishing ground-rules in class
- Asked some challenging questions of your pupils.

10 BASIC QUESTIONING SKILLS

OBJECTIVES

This chapter invites you:

- To examine a catalogue of key questioning skills
- To look at examples of these skills in practice in lessons
- To begin to put individual questioning skills into practice in your own situation.

PREPARE ... USING KEY QUESTIONS

This chapter deals with the fundamental skills we all need when we ask questions in classrooms. Often we have the skills, but perhaps rarely do we stop to analyse them. Sometimes we simply forget to make good use of them.

The first skill the teacher must remember is to plan the lesson effectively. Of course, all lessons should be planned – and most of them are. Occasionally a spontaneous opportunity arises, and a skilled teacher will know when to deviate from a plan. Ofsted inspectors still report a lack of planning in too many lessons. When questioning is used as the main vehicle of learning, what needs to be planned are the questions.

Planning a lesson for questioning is a bit tricky – but it is a knack that can be quickly learned. The aims and objectives (I prefer the word 'intentions' to cover this area) of the lesson must be identified. Then the three or four key questions that you want the students to consider.

Within each of these key question areas, you will be ready with supplementary questions to act as prompts, or to explore the issues further.

A plan for a question-based lesson might look like the one in Table 10.1. An examination of Table 10.1 shows that a whole lesson, involving some important cognitive skills (deduction and the use of evidence, reasoning, imagination, empathy, and the construction of alternative hypotheses) can be encapsulated in a question-based plan. Of

Table 10.1

An example of planning for a question-based lesson

Topic	The history of the Second World War
Theme for lesson	The evacuation and its effects on people's lives
Intentions	To help students understand the nature of evacuation – what it meant to those involved To increase their empathy with this part of the history of World War II To show that situations like this are open to a variety of opinions and attitudes, and that such situations are not clear-cut
Resources	A collection of photographs and books

Key/additional questions	**1** Why was evacuation considered so crucial to the war effort – in terms of stress? – in economic terms? – propaganda? morale? **2** Using the photographic evidence, what can you deduce about how it felt – to be an evacuee? – to have one's child(ren) evacuated? – to receive an evacuee? **3** What were the drawbacks to evacuation – for evacuees? – for their families? – for those who hosted them? – for the government? **4** What viable alternatives might there have been? What would you have done had you been a politician?
Outcome	Explore the feelings of an evacuee by reading part of Alison Prince's period piece 'How's War'
Differentiation/ Assessment	Differentiation through quality of answers to questions (teacher judgement); assessment via task in next lesson.

course, there will be many more questions asked than those listed – to encourage, probe, extend, refocus thinking and so on. But the plan contains the main elements of an intellectually demanding exercise.

USE APPROPRIATE LANGUAGE AND CONTENT

Questions are made up of words and ideas; and the students at whom they are targeted have to be able to access these in order to participate fully in the lesson. The reality of most classrooms is that they contain students of mixed levels of ability. Sometimes teachers ask: if one directs a question at an able student, surely there is a good chance that less able youngsters will not be able to understand it?

This could be true, but one of the most accessible questions one can ask is: Why? The intellectual process behind an answer to this question may be more or less complex, but the question itself is intelligible to all.

It is possible to phrase questions in complicated ways, and to use words or technical vocabulary which students cannot understand. But this is counter-productive. If the point of questioning is to get student participation, then the questions need to be phrased to achieve that end. Most teachers are aware of classroom language in the normal course of events, and transferring this awareness to questioning is no great hardship.

Activity 22

Checking the language of teacher questions

Refer to the tape you made of your questions in Activity 19. Go through the list of questions and ask yourself whether, in each case, the language and the content were appropriate. If there were complicated words or ideas, did you explain them?

If you did not make a tape in Activity 19, use the questions in the transcript quoted in Chapter 9 section 9 (above).

PROMPT AND GIVE CLUES

It was noted earlier that students have to become used to learning through questioning; and that when this method is widely used, initially students may be reluctant to answer or may feel deskilled. Because students don't always know answers, can be unwilling to offer a guess or intuitive leap, and may feel the need for extra reassurance, the teacher may have to prompt. Prompting means going back a step – or several – in the thinking process. This gives the student more chance to scaffold their learning, and a greater sense of security. The following example provides the flavour of this process.

T: What do you think are the arguments in favour of undoing the close ties between the Church and the State – what we call 'disestablishing'? Tracey?
Tracey: (No response)
T: Well, who did we say appoints Church of England bishops?
Tracey: The Prime Minister.
T: True. Is that the same as in other big organisations?
Tracey: No. The top person would – like the Archbishop or someone like that.
T: So does that strike you as odd?
Tracey: Yes. The Church should run its own affairs.
T: How might that help the Church?
John: It could be more independent.
T: Who can take John's idea a bit further?

Note how, in this transcript, the teacher fails to get a response from Tracey. However, she is anxious not to allow Tracey to feel a failure because she does not immediately know an answer. So she leads the student back through a series of logical steps, going over some ideas that have already been expressed, until Tracey can articulate a useful comment. At that point, so as not to exclude others, the teacher quickly brings in another respondent to sustain group involvement, and moves the discussion back to the wider audience.

Prompting is a way of keeping up the questioning process when it might otherwise falter, and doing this by back-tracking and using clues is a way of keeping student participation maximised.

DISTRIBUTE QUESTIONS AROUND THE CLASS

In the last brief transcript of classroom questioning we saw how the teacher had to pause for a while to bring on the thinking and understanding of one pupil, but how she was able to return quite speedily to involve the whole group. This is a rather specialised example of the skill to which we now turn in this section.

To be effective, questions have to be well targeted and everyone in the learning group has to be involved in answering. The teacher must retain an awareness all the time of two important classroom events:

- what the students are learning (through feedback to the teacher's questions and the quality of the responses); and
- which students are involved and which are uninvolved.

There are some very simple class management techniques that can help in the distribution of questions around the class. The first is to consider the arc of vision. In Figure 10.1 there are two diagrams showing teachers talking to students. By a simple movement to a new position relative to the student group, the second teacher is able to gain a better view of the group. This in turn means that it is easier for him or her to target questions to specific pupils, to watch reactions to the questions and to the answers given by other students, and to keep proper discipline in the group if necessary.

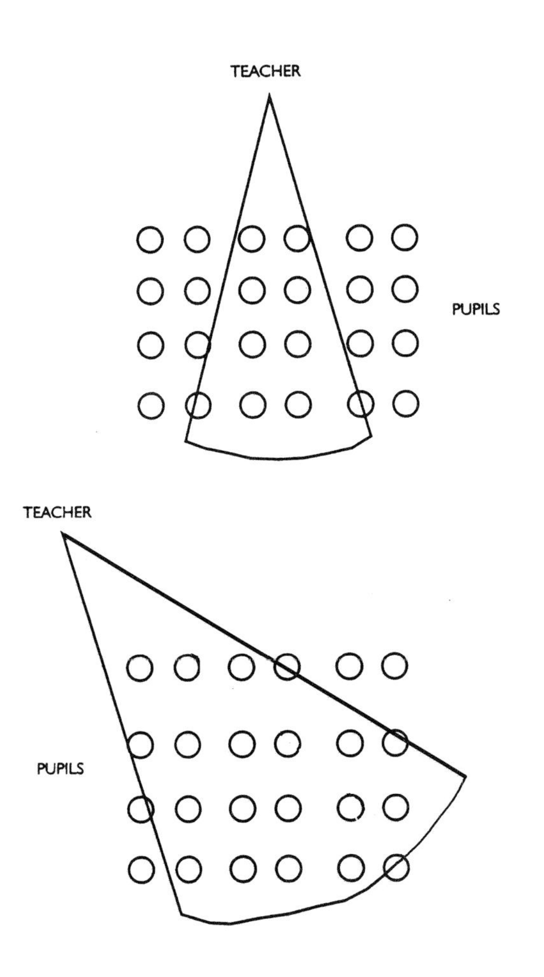

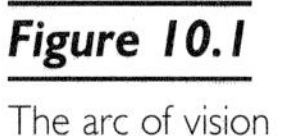

The arc of vision

Figure 10.2

Zones of involvement

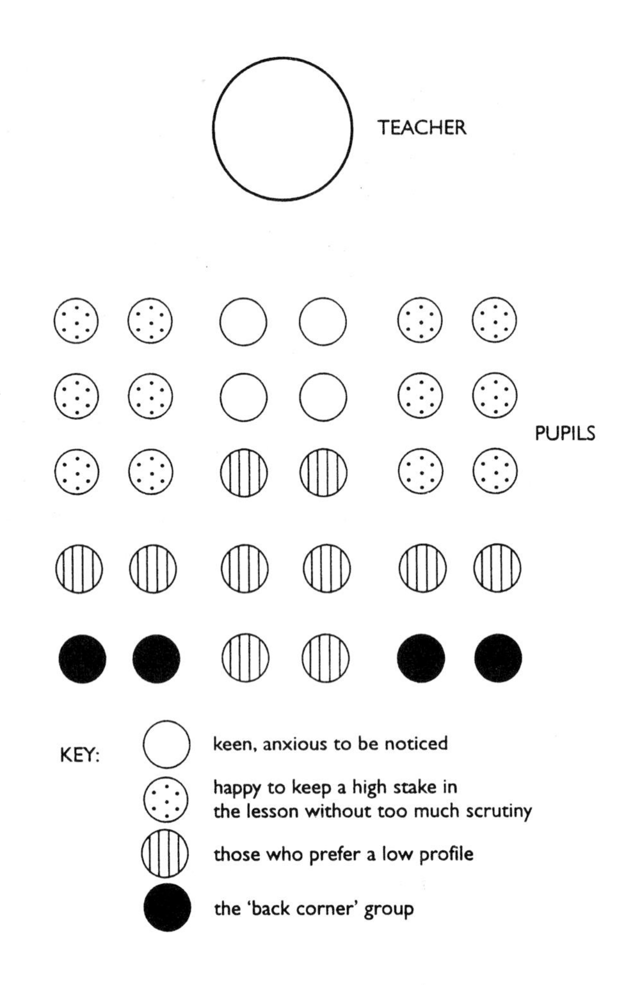

Figure 10.2 suggests that where students sit within the room may give a broad signal about their preferred learning relation to the teacher. Those who dominate the front of the room may also dominate answering, and therefore the interaction that takes place in the classroom. Conversely, those out of sight at the back may avoid involvement – even in quite small groups. Ideally the teacher will want to make sure that everyone participates and so they should keep the initiative of vision and vigilance.

When eager students are bursting to answer, and a forest of hands means that the teacher is spoilt for choice of respondent, there is a converse temptation to ask the one or two who do not offer a reply. This often puts undue pressure and embarrassment on them, which, in turn, is counterproductive, because they will be even more unwilling in the future if they feel their responses are inadequate. It is sometimes necessary to draw a student in deliberately; but it is always better to watch for an eye-contact or gesture (a nod, a smile) which suggests that there may be a response available, however modest the student may be about offering it.

Activity 23

Distributing questions

In this Activity you should teach a question-based lesson to a reasonably large student group. Tape the lesson, or a proportion of it (about 30 minutes' duration), or get someone to observe you and make notes.

When you have the opportunity, play back the tape and try to note the number of students offering responses to your questions.

How many times did each reply?

Was anyone dominant?

Did any student not participate?

(Alternatively, you can get a colleague to watch the lesson, to record the kinds of information described above, and to feed back the data and their impressions after the event.)

USE STUDENT RESPONSES – EVEN WRONG ONES!

I once sat and watched a PSE lesson in which an 'expert' at question-based teaching – a huge extrovert man – was trying to get a group of Y11 students to talk about issues to do with unemployment. The group was a bit diffident, dominated by the few keen respondents. One student did not make any comment for about 40 minutes: a small, shy girl who had mobility problems. Finally, the teacher rounded on her noisily and demanded: 'Marlene, how much do you think you get if you're on the dole?'

Surprised, Marlene stuttered an absurdly low figure – she had no idea! 'What a stupid answer', bellowed the teacher, banging the table in mock horror; and everyone laughed.

The embarrassment of the youngster, and mine, are still engraved on my soul.

In a way, describing how not to use wrong answers – however irritating – is easier than describing how to use them. One of the most frequent methods is for the teacher to gloss over them with a 'damned with faint praise' approach that fools no one:

T: When was the Battle of Hastings fought?
Daren: 1257, Miss.
T: Well, you're not too far out, Daren. Does anyone . . .?

This example is only a slight caricature.

The trick is to be able to say that the answer is wrong, and to point the respondent towards a better one, at the same time.

T: In the book, why was the boy How attracted to the big house?
Julie: He wanted to live in it.
T: No, Julie, you're getting confused. You want to live in a big house. How went there because of some information. What was that?

This approach is akin to the 'prompt and give clues' procedure discussed earlier.

Time questions and pause between them

At training days on questioning, I often ask audience members to say whether they would wait longer for an answer to one of their questions from the most able pupil in the class or from the least able. It's a trick question – like how long is a piece of string? The circumstances, subject matter, and knowledge of the pupil all make a difference. But ... there is a serious point to it. Both pupils need thinking time – the pause between the question and the answer. The most able pupils need it because they are preparing a mini-dissertation in their heads; and the least able need it because it takes them a long time to formulate a relatively simple response. Of course, all the other students need thinking time, too.

Pausing between questions, then, provides that vital second or two – perhaps a little longer – when the thoughts start to flow and get themselves sorted out, sequenced and then vocalised. The amazing thing is that it happens as quickly as it does! Think back to the last job interview you had: you needed to compose your answers – yet the questions seemed to come thick and fast. So maybe you invented a few ploys to give yourself those vital moments. Perhaps you began an answer with a safe, mildly humorous remark as your serious thoughts formed; maybe you just spent a moment moving position in your seat to face the questioner; or smiled in knowing concentration for a moment while you controlled the start of your reply. We all invent these little ploys for gaining thinking time – and students need them, too.

The aim of the skilled questioner is to help students to know that thinking time is available – to signal that a thoughtful answer is better than a quick, glib response. We do this through the use of praise, or the body language we use to show interest – just as we do spontaneously outside the class in what we call conversation. But, unlike in conversation, we may have to explain the purpose of the pause to a class and give reasons for it.

But there is another art in which pausing is useful: the art of emphasis or of surprise. If, as the dialogue between students and teacher progresses, the teacher can build in good timing of (effective) questions to keep interest sustained, then the lesson will be more productive. It is the same art as the comedian uses to tell jokes: listen to a professional comedian and you quickly discover that it is not the words that are funny, often not just the ideas, but the impact of the punch-line after a pause. As professional communicators, teachers need to use the tricks of the trade!

Make progressive cognitive demands

The final section in this chapter of basic skills returns to the theme of cognitive demand. You may find it helpful to revisit page 71 *et seq*.

In Chapter 8 the questions which were labelled 'higher order' questions comprised:

- application questions – often 'How?'questions
- analytical questions – often 'Why?' questions
- questions requiring synthesis – 'What light does our knowledge of geography throw on this historical event?'
- evaluation questions – 'What makes x better than y?'

It was suggested that, over time in a lesson, the teacher needed to increase the proportion of questions requiring higher order thinking. With this in mind, the final Activity in this chapter asks you to put together several of the skills referred to in the chapter in preparation for teaching a lesson. You will practise higher order questions again in the next chapter.

Activity 24

Putting questioning skills together

This Activity asks you to combine the skills of preparing using key questions; of building cognitive demand during a lesson through your questions; and of pausing between, and timing, questions effectively.

Again, you need to record the lesson or part of the lesson. Plan your lesson as suggested above (page 84).

In your planning make sure that the questions you use have a progressive cognitive demand, perhaps starting with a few low order questions, or returning to these when you need to prompt. As you teach, try quite consciously to build in thinking time for students before accepting the first response. (If necessary brief the class on the value of formulating thoughtful answers.)

Later, go over the tape and assess your performance. What problems did you encounter? What would you do differently next time?

Activity 24 is an exercise which you may have to repeat several times before you become sufficiently self-aware to control the processes without the support of a taped analysis afterwards.

Outcomes

At the end of this chapter you should have:

- Understood the main components of questioning skills
- Improved the register of language in which you frame classroom questions
- Become more aware of the skill of distributing questions around the class
- Practised putting a number of skills together during a lesson, especially with a view to raising the cognitive demand of questions.

---

11 Higher order questions revisited

OBJECTIVES

This chapter invites you:

- To revisit the issue of higher order questioning in order to understand it more fully
- To examine in more detail each of the six kinds of questions identified in this book
- To consider examples of each question type in relation to subject areas

This book has placed a good deal of emphasis so far on the intellectual performance of students in classrooms. It has suggested that taking the intuitive leap is to be encouraged, that problem-solving should be central to teaching style, and that questions should make progressive cognitive demands on students. Both Chapters 8 and 10 have looked in a cursory way at higher order questions. This chapter tries to take this last issue a little further.

For a number of years I have classified questions using an adapted form of the Bloom model, and this has proved invaluable as a way of testing the intellectual demands of classrooms. This chapter looks at each of the question types featured in that adapted model, and attempts both to illustrate them and to indicate circumstances in which these kinds of questions can be valuable.

Recall questions

Recall questions are low order, but are the most frequent of all classroom questions. Examples are:

- Do you remember what we were talking about last time?
- How many legs did we say a spider had?
- Which day of the week, did we discover, was named after the old god Thor?
- How did we set out a sum like this?
- What did we call a valley which had contours like this?
- When was it that we said we would use this formula?

What these questions share is the fact that they are all designed to help students recall or revise material which has already been covered – hence the label. They are the staple diet of classroom questioning. They are useful as a starting point to a session or a topic because they focus the student's mind on the subject matter before the teacher tries to move on. The problem is that they dominate classroom questioning while making relatively low intellectual demand.

Of course, there are those who will immediately argue that it is inevitable that this type of questioning dominates, since most students are not really that bright, or that motivated, that the issues under discussion are not foremost in their minds and in their consciousness. These teachers will see every lesson as a kind of battle – a battle against lack of interest, or against lack of ability, or against lack of enthusiasm. This is a view that is open to challenge.

It could also be argued, with some conviction, that the reason there is so much apathy in (some) classrooms (particularly, it is suggested in the White Paper 2001, Key Stage 3 classes) is precisely because the work is not adequately challenging and does not, therefore, capture students' imaginations. The problem lies not in the use of recall questions, but in their overuse, or in their use to the exclusion of other kinds of question. In fact, it could be suggested that the use of more demanding work would actually increase motivation and participation – and this is a view which this book adopts.

Nevertheless, it is a natural instinct of the teacher to want to establish some common intellectual ground, some shared knowledge, with students before the lesson moves on. Recall questions are valuable in serving that function: and so their use is to be welcomed. But, there are probably ground-rules for their use which would make them more effective:

- don't start *every* session with a set of recall questions to establish the starting point: vary the method with other ploys – see Activity 25
- limit the number of recall questions at the beginning of a session to three or four at the most
- keep your own contributions (such as comments on answers) as brief as possible.

Activity 25

Finding alternatives to recall questions

Many lessons require to be started by ensuring that students can remember things that were learned in the previous session.

Think of as many ways as you can to achieve this aim without asking a set of recall questions.

Use these other methods, too, in your own teaching.

(Some possible solutions to this Activity are listed at the end of the chapter.)

Recall questions are also used during lessons, as a means for the teacher to obtain feedback on how learning is progressing. This is an entirely proper phenomenon, and feedback is a vital part of the teaching process. Similar ground-rules to those already listed probably apply. The key is not to overuse them in these circumstances either.

Recall questions, then, have a place in classroom questioning but they are low order questions and can tend to stifle the higher order questions we are looking for to raise the cognitive demand. For this reason they should be used sparingly, and perhaps as a not-too-frequent alternative to other methods of revision and reinforcement – particularly at the beginning of lessons.

Comprehension questions

This category is a more controversial one. The controversy centres mainly on the definition of 'comprehension'. Some would argue that comprehension is a higher order skill, and that questions of this type should be included with higher order, rather than low order, questions. The Bloomian model tends to support this view. My adapted model does not.

The problem with comprehension questions as they are asked in the real world of classroom teaching is that they rarely imply any higher order thought! While the Bloomian approach is absolutely correct as a theoretical model, in practice teachers use questions of this kind as revision and reinforcement. But the answers require only regurgitation, not intellectual building-on. Typical examples would be:

- So, looking at the example we just used as a model, what would '*x*' be in this equation?
- The passage we have just read suggested where the best tea was grown: where was that?
- The story gave some important clues, so who can tell me what Adrian's mood was like on that day?
- We covered this ground yesterday, so what is the missing word here?

In deciding whether a question is higher order or not, one of the most important clues is in the expected or desired answer. In the examples above it is clear that revision of known material is required – and that does not advance the cognitive demand. For that reason I would normally classify these questions as low order. Nevertheless, I would concede that it is possible to ask higher order comprehension questions:

- If you were an American Indian who believed that gods lived in every tree, how would you view the clearing of your forest?

Assuming that the teacher had not provided the answer in what had gone before, this question does ask the student to make a deduction – and that is a higher order skill.

For practical purposes one needs to be aware of this tension in classifying comprehension questions, but we shall continue to call them low order questions in this book because many are. The remainder we can transfer to other classifications of higher order questions, such as the four which follow.

APPLICATION QUESTIONS

Questions of this type ask students to understand a general principle and then apply it. Examples might include:

- (In PE) How could you improve your time around this circuit?
- (In history) Given your knowledge of the terrain, where would you build the castle?
- (In RE) How might early humans have begun to move towards an idea of God or gods?
- (In maths) What formula would we apply to a problem like this?
- (In English) How might we begin to compose our own haiku?

Application questions take us unambiguously into the world of increasing cognitive demand. They are characterised by being 'open'. They ask students to take information and then to manipulate it (by applying it) as opposed to merely regurgitating it. This process of manipulation is the crucial one in assessing whether or not there is cognitive demand. If one wanted, one could regard this as the 'value-added' element in the learning – the 'going beyond the given'.

Application questions – or the potential to use them – are universal across all subject areas. There are a myriad opportunities in classrooms to formulate these questions. Almost every time new ground is covered by the students (i.e. new knowledge acquired), there is the potential for extension into application (and thereby, for achieving a measure of understanding). The answers may contain what we called 'intuitive leaps' – and these should be encouraged.

Nor is application the domain only of the more able. All pupils enjoy and benefit from the notion of seeing 'how it works in practice'.

It is an important question type in providing feedback to teachers: they can assess the acquired understanding, as opposed to checking only on knowledge and the potential for repetition. In classrooms one has always to be aware of the 'Long John's parrot' syndrome. The parrot could repeat important phrases, but had no understanding of, or use for, them. They lacked meaning for the parrot. Education of students has to aim rather higher than this – to raise the cognitive stakes.

Application questions should be a staple diet of classroom life, a feature of every lesson and of all new material – a part of the process of challenge and a cornerstone of the problem-solving approach to learning.

Activity 26

Practising the use of application questions

Choose a lesson when you intend to introduce some new material to a class.

Present the material using an appropriate method. Plan to follow up your presentation with a problem or problems which have to be solved by applying the new principles.

Prepare your application questions, and pose these problems to the class.

Keep notes on the session. For example, how enthusiastically did the students respond? How well did they complete the task? What could be done better next time? What were the successes of the session? Did (some of) the students exceed your expectations? How?

ANALYSIS QUESTIONS

Another good question type for raising cognitive demand is the analysis question. The trademark of these questions is the word: Why?

- (In maths) Why is it important to write figures down in neat columns when we are dealing with large numbers like hundreds, tens and units?
- (In RE) Why did Moses feel so angry when he saw the slave being beaten?
- (In English) Why does the author give her characters such strange names?
- (In geography) Why do we know that the hill at this point is very steep?

But also . . .

- (In history) Can you think of three reasons why this enterprise was doomed to failure?
- (In music) What is the composer's purpose in selecting these particular instruments to play this phrase?
- (In technology) What is it about the design of this advert that holds the attention?

The thought processes involved in answering analysis questions are:

- to break the subject down into parts
- to reflect on the nature of those parts, and
- to study the inter-relations between the parts.

This type of question, like the application question, goes beyond given data and requires the student to build on existing knowledge. There may be elements of hypothesis or the intuitive leap involved. Certainly, the student will have to make the problem their own. The language of analysis questions may be deceptively simple but the intellectual demand can be high, and may be interpreted by the more able at a very high level while still 'stretching' the average and less able.

Again, there may be some objection from some teachers that this technique is too difficult for the less able students in the class. However, 'Why?' questions imply a problem-solving approach, and all pupils can benefit from this. The science teacher who generates in students the attitude that science is about being detectives – one looks for clues, collates the evidence, and draws conclusions – is likely to have more committed students than the teacher who dictates both the problem and the answer using the blackboard or even a multicoloured worksheet. Teachers often stress – and even politicians appear persuaded by – the need for students to grow to love the subject they are studying. The excitement of analysis is a contributory factor in the excitement that leads to commitment.

Of course, there are dangers in analysis. People – of any age – who do a lot of analysis do develop a tendency to challenge everything. Just occasionally this leads to friction in schools. A classic case which I came across was of a musician who used this technique frequently. The students became very questioning about everything in his lessons, and, while he was totally at home with this, when the technique spilled over into other lessons some colleagues became aggressive. The poor musician was effectively 'sent to Coventry' by his colleagues, who regarded him as a dangerous maverick who had a subversive influence on young minds! It was a good job that hemlock was in short supply in that town or he might have been forced to drink it.

Good teachers should never be afraid of an intellectual challenge from students, and should welcome and praise it. Only through enquiry are great strides made for humankind.

QUESTIONS REQUIRING SYNTHESIS

It is quite hard to define synthesis, but in my adapted version of the Bloomian model I use this category to describe the taking of an idea from one context and reapplying it in another, rather different, context. To give an example of synthesis at work one might consider a conventional mathematics lesson. In it the student learns how to express data in graphic form: what the axes of a graph are, how to plot against criteria on the two axes, how to link the plots, and how to interpret the resulting line or curve. Later, in science, the teacher sets a problem (say, to measure how quickly water cools); and the students are asked to write a table of results. Some of them use a graphical form in which to encapsulate their data, and the resultant plots as a means to expressing their findings. The students have synthesised learning in one area by applying it in another.

So synthesis questions might include examples like these:

- (In RE) How can a knowledge of demographic trends help to throw light on this moral problem?
- (In English) How might the views put across in this novel affect your attitudes towards medical research?
- (In science) Can you think of anything you have learned about rocks which might help to tell us something about this fossil creature?

If one of the outcomes of analysis questions is to build a love of the subject matter, then one of the outcomes of synthesis as a questioning approach is to build bridges between subjects and pieces of discrete knowledge within subjects. This is almost exclusively a higher order process. Interestingly enough, when research has been carried out into questioning and higher order thinking demand, it has tended to show that teachers in primary schools, and teachers in secondary schools working in integrated areas such as humanities, ask a greater proportion of higher order questions than other teachers. The secret to this finding is in the links themselves – the inevitable How? and Why? questions of inter-connection. These differences in cognitive demand between groups of teachers have been at very high levels of significance, emphasising the crucial nature both of synthesis questions and of making cross-curricular links. After all, in real life knowledge is not divided into neat, time-tabled, subject areas, is it?

EVALUATION QUESTIONS

The final category of higher order questions on which this chapter will throw a spotlight is that of evaluation questions.

Evaluation questions are easy to define and to exemplify. They ask pupils to make judgements and define the reasons for those judgements:

- (In mathematics) So, of the three ways I have shown you, which do you think is the best one for calculating the areas of these figures?
- (In English) What makes this a successful novel?
- (In science) Given that this part of the country is quite windy, which of these methods of seed dispersal do you think is most likely to be successful for plants growing here?
- (In geography) Given the clues on the map, which of these pieces of terrain is going to be easier to cross?
- (In history) Who was the better general: Montgomery or Rommel?
- (In technology) Can you say which fabric is best for the purpose?

Evaluation questions, by definition, tend to be very open questions. They usually require the use of evidence and reasoning, and this puts them into the higher order of cognitive demand. They also expect the student to compare and contrast, to produce a possibly balanced answer not just a snap judgement. They can often be followed with a 'Why?' question, which asks the student to justify the answer by revealing how they came to their conclusion.

Though this is strictly a different topic, to be dealt with in another book, evaluation questions are often at the heart of written questions such as those in public examination papers. They are, therefore, important in the classroom as a way of preparing students for other contexts in which they will have to think and perform effectively.

SUMMARY

One of the declared aims of this book is to assist the teacher to increase the proportion of higher order questions asked in comparison to low order ones. This chapter has examined question types in more detail, and in particular has looked at the nature of four kinds of higher order questions. The next task, in Activity 27, is to try to pursue asking higher order questions more frequently in your own lessons.

Activity 27

Preparing higher order questions

When you sit down to plan your lessons for a complete week, build into the plan for each lesson at least three higher order questions.

Try to ensure that you use each of the question types:

- Application
- Analysis
- Synthesis
- Evaluation.

Keep brief notes on how effective the questions were: in particular, whether they sparked ideas and interest in ways which you did not anticipate.

And finally, here are some possible solutions relating to Activity 25:

1 Use a two-minute, self-marked, test
2 Try a piece of cloze material
3 Have key points from last time already written up on the blackboard, white-board or OHP
4 Ask a student to rehearse the key points of the last lesson
5 Go over the key issues yourself, verbally and quickly
6 Use a handout
7 Use method 2 or 3 above, but this time build in one or two errors and ask the class to 'spot the deliberate mistakes'.

Outcomes

At the end of this chapter you should have:

- Understood the different kinds of higher order questions, their definitions and functions for raising cognition in classes
- Practised your own use of higher order questions in your lessons.

---

12 STUDENTS CAN ASK QUESTIONS TOO!

OBJECTIVES

This chapter invites you:

- To investigate the questions pupils ask
- To consider the place of student questions in lessons
- To reflect on how to deal with pupils' questions
- To begin to develop a 'questioning class' approach to your groups.

The exclamation mark in the title of this chapter relates to an assertion made by Dillon (1988) about the questions students ask (or don't ask):

> *For, as a rule, students do not ask questions. There is little room for their questions in normal practice, and little rhyme or reason for them to ask. They are busied with other things, notably giving answers to teacher questions. Classroom discourse normally proceeds in ways that rule out student questions, while other powerful conditions and facts of life give students good reasons not to ask. With most odds against them asking, students understandably ask few questions. (p. 7)*

This assertion may not ring as true to a British educator as it does to an American; we may be dealing with cultural differences here. But my guess is that most teachers in Britain would not agree with this overall assertion; and that most British classrooms would not support Dillon's view. (Having said that, Wragg's (1993) Leverhulme Project did throw up the same concern: in 20 lessons observed only 20 questions were asked by the primary pupils involved. This does not ring true either to my own experience as a researcher or to my still current experience in primary classrooms.)

It might be more informative for us to ponder on what kinds of questions students ask.

Activity 28

Finding out about student questions

Use a tape recorder or a notebook to record or jot down all the student questions which occur during a morning or an afternoon in class. Later, try to classify the questions into categories like those below (you may have to form your own categories based on the kinds of questions you have noted). Questions which:

- ask administrative things (can I get more paper?)
- ask for clarification of your instructions
- ask for clarification of information contained in the lesson
- pursue the understanding of the conceptual material
- introduce new issues to the lesson
- are 'red herrings'.

Your mini-survey in Activity 28 will tell you something unique about your own classroom and about the ways in which students question you. The findings should give you some clues about your own teaching. For example, if a significant proportion of the questions were 'red herrings' then maybe you need to look at your class management techniques. If most were clarification of your instructions, then perhaps you are not giving clear and sequenced guidelines. Similarly, if there are a lot of questions which suggest the students have understood well beyond the scope of your planned lesson, perhaps you are pitching material at too low a level; or, if these questions emanate from one student, perhaps that individual is outstandingly able and needs differentiated work.

All of these insights may be supported from your survey, but these are not the main issues for this chapter. Here, we are concerned with what the teacher can do to deal with student questions most effectively. Of course, it helps you, in your unique situation, to know what messages these questions are delivering, but the chapter is concerned more with principles than with specifics.

PLAN INTO LESSONS TIME FOR STUDENT QUESTIONS

If Dillon's assertion contains some truth – and it probably does – then we have to ask ourselves why there are fewer student questions than might benefit the learning in our classes. The most likely explanation might well be that teachers simply don't plan in enough time for them, and therefore don't encourage them. There is always a pressure on the curriculum, and that pressure tends to push teachers towards talking a lot in order to do what they tend to describe as 'covering the ground'. Curriculum pressure in secondary settings tends to refer to public examinations – even when these are years away. But both Key Stage 2 and Key Stage 3 teachers feel the pressure of SATs; and ultimately, of course, of league tables. The National Curriculum is certainly cast as villain by the majority of teachers who comment on this problem. However, we have seen that the fact of teaching is not a guarantee of learning, and the student involvement in learning is vital for its success. Student questions are one way through which that involvement (including interest and motivation) might be achieved.

The message, then, has to be that in time-planning for lessons the option for student questions, and for dealing with them effectively, has to be taken seriously.

STUDENT QUESTIONS MUST BE WELCOMED

One of the early principles established in this book was that as teachers we ought to want our students to talk – but to talk constructively and on-task. Questions are a manifestation of that talk. Student questions indicate an engagement with the material being taught, and so are an important indicator of intellectual commitment.

Whether or not students will be willing to ask questions, and continue to do so, depends on the trust which is built up between teacher and learner. How often have you heard in classes:

- 'Don't ask such stupid questions.'
- 'I haven't got time to answer that now.'
- 'You talk too much, Sam.'
- 'I've told you once, Just get on! . . .'

and so on?

Sometimes, these are legitimate remarks – sometimes. But just review your own practice honestly, and see if you stifle contribution rather than welcome it.

ENCOURAGE STUDENT QUESTIONS AS A WAY OF LEARNING

One certain way to keep questions coming is to signal their importance by making use of them. This includes making them welcome – but goes further than this. In the next Activity you are invited to think of some ways in which student questions can be built into the lesson process.

Activity 29

Finding ways to encourage student questions

How can you build student questions into your lessons?

Your strategies might include ways of using questions which arise spontaneously, and also ways of encouraging students to formulate questions in more systematic ways.

Make a list of possible strategies in your notebook, and then set about trying them out, one at a time, as circumstances permit.

Some ideas are given at the end of the chapter – only consult these when you have invented a few methods of your own.

LISTEN TO THE QUESTIONS STUDENTS ASK

This may seem a pretty obvious thing to say, but the fact is that teachers are much more expert at talking than listening. We all need to develop the skill to listen – but in this case we are talking about listening on a variety of levels:

- paying attention
- hearing the question itself

- gaining clues about any hidden motive in the asking, for example, insecurity about technical language
- being sensitive to student opinions (for example, in the area of controversial subjects like health, the student may have personal worries)
- listening for misunderstandings.

In listening to the question, one of the skills may be not just to formulate a brilliant response. Teachers tend to assume that the best way to deal with a student's question is always to answer it in a neat, succinct way. In fact, the student may be better encouraged to pursue the question him/herself through a series of teacher questions that set up an analytical or probing process for the questioner – a process akin to our advice that the student should be made to own classroom problems. Other students may be able to be encouraged to join the debate.

Sometimes, the class response to a student question may be one of scorn or boredom – other students may know, or think they know, the answer. It is hard to prevent this 'switching off' process, but you should try. The respect factor is important here: and fellow students may be subtly guided to see that the first question may not be the ultimate one – their colleague's real difficulty may be more complicated, and they may even share it!

Remember, in signalling your interest or otherwise in the questions posed by students the biggest giveaway is not what you say. You are more likely to convey boredom or frustration by tone than in your spoken words. More often, you will control both of these: but your body language will give you away. You may sigh, raise your eyebrows, look at the clock, do another job (such as giving out papers) while answering – and so on. These cryptic signals will have a negative effect on future exchanges.

A QUESTIONING CLASS

What has been said so far in the chapter suggests that students' questions should be encouraged and sustained. In this Dillon makes five important points that are worth rehearsal and commentary.

The first is that the teacher should reward the perplexity that generates the question. By this he means that too much emphasis is placed, in normal circumstances, on what he calls 'the procession through the subject matter' (*op. cit.* p. 31). Instead, the teacher needs to signal pleasure at the engagement of the student with the underlying issues of it. What Dillon is really describing here is what we might label the learning environment. There are a number of factors that go to make up an effective learning environment:

- the physical factors (such as the layout of the room, ensuring that everyone can see and hear, or that there are stimulating display materials)

- the psychological factors, ensuring that students feel secure and able to say what it is they want to say, and
- the cognitive factors – the conviction from experience of the students that this classroom is about sharing knowledge, problems and solutions which are jointly owned by the teacher and the students themselves.

Dillon's second point is that the teacher must help the students to understand that they can empower themselves to know; and this book would add 'to understand'. They do not have to appeal to the teacher as an authority for a ready-made answer. This is harder than many teachers allow for. Even today, teachers are seen as authority figures – at least in the realms of subject matter. Society, as well as students, expects the teacher to know, and to say what they know. This attitude goes back to a deep-seated (and, arguably, false) belief that knowledge (as opposed to understanding) is at the heart of the education process. Sadly, it is a view that has dogged English education from its earliest times, and which from time to time is reinforced and given credence by political pronouncements. In England, the schoolmaster (in history it was usually the *schoolmaster*) was often almost the only literate member of the community, and as such was appealed to in this 'fount of all wisdom' way. Old habits die hard, and it is not uncommon even now for this attitude to prevail in rural areas, despite almost universal literacy.

Dillon's third point repeats what was said earlier in this chapter: that the question asked may not be the question that is really troubling the student. The teacher needs to be aware of that, and to use the probing skills described earlier to try to uncover the underlying perplexities or concerns.

Fourth, Dillon encourages the teacher to explore, in collaboration with the student, these underlying questions: there must be an element of feedback questioning (to probe the student's understanding), and of probing to help further future improved understanding.

The final tactic is to use the first four strategies as ways of sustaining a dialogue with the student, rather than ending the conversation or discussion. In doing this the teacher makes an implicit statement to the class that this process of questioning and exploration is important to all of them and to the learning process.

Woods (1993) argues that students learn most effectively from what he calls 'critical events' in the classroom. Such critical events might be the production of a video or an exciting project. In my own school I asked a mixture of Y3 to Y6 students who were studying the Greeks as part of their National Curriculum syllabus to compile a Greek newspaper of the time. We decided that it had to have all the normal features of a modern newspaper, that it had to be produced against a deadline, that different students would play different roles (editor, picture editor, reporters of various kinds), and that it had to have an audience – in our case parents waiting at the school door for their children to emerge at the end of the school day.

Critical events like this share certain key characteristics – in particular they start with a good idea, which may come from the students; there is an 'explosion stage' in which this idea is expanded through considering the creative possibilities; there is consolidation as the work is done; and there is celebration in the products that are generated.

My contention would be that student questions will sometimes, perhaps often, fall into this category of a critical event. The skill is to recognise them, and then to make something happen from them. There is some evidence that, post-National Curriculum, teachers and head-teachers are reluctant to travel these roads: but our professionalism demands that we do, and that we can articulate why we do.

Activity 30

Capitalising on student questions

Seek out an opportunity, using one your strategies from Activity 29, to encourage your students to generate questions for you.

Give the students the chance to put the questions.

Record the session, if possible.

From the recording, or from your memory of what happened, try to assess the relevance, scope and quality of what took place.

What was successful?

What would you do differently next time?

Some suggestions relating to Activity 29:

1 Build investigations – as opposed to presentation of explanations or answers – into your lessons.
2 End the lesson with a question for the students to ponder, informally, before next time.
3 Learn from the TV soap operas: have some threads of the lesson which carry over until next time.
4 Construct tasks for pupils that ask them to devise questions rather than answer them.
5 Even in reinforcement exercises it is possible for you to engage students in teams, pairs, etc., in which one (group) poses questions to the other (group) as a way of starting dialogue.
6 Occasionally, tell the students what the subject of the next lesson will be – and request that they come prepared with questions to ask you rather than you feeding them information.
7 Use homework as a time, for example, to support idea 6 above.
8 Introduce a kind of 'time-out' system between parts of your explanations in where there is an interval in which students can ask questions of you.

Outcomes

At the end of this chapter you should have:

- Become more aware of pupils' questions
- Investigated the kinds of questions pupils ask
- Begun to make more time for pupils' questions in lessons
- Developed better listening skills
- Developed pupils' questioning into a tool for learning.

REFERENCES

Dillon, James T. (1988) *Questioning and Teaching: A Manual of Practice*. London: Croom Helm.
Woods, P. (1993). *Critical Events in Teaching and Learning*. London: Falmer Press.
Wragg, E.C. (1993) *Questioning*. London: Routledge.

THINGS TO AVOID WHEN QUESTIONING

13

OBJECTIVES

This chapter invites you:

- To consider some of the errors teachers make when using questioning as a learning medium
- To raise awareness of aspects of your own behaviour that may inhibit your effectiveness as a questioner.

I was once present at a conference at which a variety of adult education trainers were explaining how they taught their students in vocational settings. The hotel chef talked about incentive bonuses for good performance, and the police instructor described experiments in mentoring young constables on paired beats. Then the Army representatives stood up. Their opening was not a word but a picture: a famous shot of a graveyard in the Falklands. The major said, 'We only get one chance to get it right.' It was a very powerful message.

Luckily, mistakes in teaching are rarely fatal. (Having said that, I once marked an examination paper from a developing country in which the candidate was asked to discuss the relationship between the school and the community. He noted that a local principal had failed to take account of the community's wishes, 'so they mutilated him'.)

It is often as effective to learn from mistakes – one's own and other people's – as it is to learn from guidelines, models or exhortations. In this chapter we shall be taking the negative view in order to gain some positive messages. Our task now is to look at some of the common errors in questioning, and to try to take from them the positive skills that are implicit in not making these mistakes. So what are the common errors that teachers make when using classroom questions?

INAPPROPRIATE MARRIAGE

One of the commonest errors in trying to use classroom questions is when the teacher has not thought out effectively the relation between this method of learning and the material to be presented. There can be no doubt that some material (such as problem-based issues) is relatively easily converted via key questions into a lesson based on questioning. Other kinds of material (perhaps the introduction of new technical terms at the start of a fresh module of work) may lend themselves more readily towards didactic methods, handouts or access through a visual aid.

In theory, almost everything taught in the class could be question-based: it is just a matter of manipulating the content into a suitable format. But one should bear in mind two factors:

- efficiency, and
- variety.

Some teachers would argue quite powerfully that there are times when one can cover a substantial stretch of the syllabus quickly and efficiently through a presentation. By contrast, it is argued, the question-based approach can be quite slow.

My own view is that this is a fair argument, and combined with the need for variety in methods of classroom working it presents a valid point of view. If all classroom work were based on the questioning/problem-solving approach it would produce a possibly stimulating, but rather predictable, diet of work for youngsters. Part of the aim of every teacher must be to switch teaching methods in order to sustain interest. There is also the fact that within a class of 30 or so students some will respond to one teaching method best, others to quite a different method. This marriage – often referred to as matching – between preferred learning styles of students and preferred teaching styles of teachers is very important. The particular blend of methods you choose, along with your approach to class management and the ethos of learning you create, are the factors that go to make up your particular and unique teaching style.

So the rule must be to match questioning sessions to the kind of material from the syllabus which most lends itself to this approach, while remaining aware that questioning puts the responsibility for learning on students – and that should be a daily classroom intention.

POOR PREPARATION

Another failure in questioning lessons is where the teacher has not prepared using the key questions and supplementary questions referred to in Chapter 10.

All lessons need preparation; but when using questions one has to be aware of the variety of directions in which students may take off, and be ready both to follow productive leads and to draw their answers back if they become diverted from the main topic.

Though one tends to assume that most classroom lessons are prepared, the fact is that Ofsted inspectors report that evidence of preparation is often lacking. I have certainly witnessed teachers who, consistently and chronically, fail to do any short-term planning or preparation. This is a serious fault: and its outcome is usually that students' work has to be kept to very predictable exercises and the teacher's inputs to didactic sessions to support the exercises. Only in this way can the teacher retain control of the syllabus. This attitude won't work when using a questioning and problem-solving approach to learning.

FAILURE OF VOICE CONTROL

Teachers talk a lot: the ability to **use** the voice – not just to speak – is very important.

Students receive a multiplicity of signals through the teacher's voice: signals about enthusiasm, control, direction of thought, humour, the light and shade of a lesson – what is more, and what is less, important. There is nothing more off-putting than a teacher whose voice control is poor. No matter what the content, and how brilliant the teaching strategies, students will tune out. The common faults are:

- lack of expression
- a hectoring style
- too high a pitch.

DISTRIBUTION

Another fault concerns the distribution of questions around the class. Again, we looked at the positive things about this in an earlier chapter. The common problems with distribution of questions tend to centre on the unconscious behaviour of the teacher:

- unconscious gender bias
- targeting students as a means of class control only (rather than getting full attention first)
- bias towards asking the most able
- bias towards those who offer answers
- failure to notice non-participants
- targeting open questions to the able, and only the closed ones to the less able.

Teaching is a busy occupation, and it is easy to lose track of our behaviour as we teach. An exercise such as Activity 31 is often useful to highlight any bad habits we have acquired.

Activity 31

Analysing distribution patterns

Find an opportunity during which a trusted colleague can watch one of your question-based lessons.

Ask them to observe your distribution of questions around the class using a grid like the one below.

Afterwards, try to discuss together your pattern of distributing questions: does it contain any bias?

Remember: because you are aware of being observed you will probably perform more self-consciously than you would normally, so emergent problems may be more pronounced in reality than they appear as a result of this exercise.

Observing the distribution of questions around the class

No.	Question	Target
Q.1	What is milk?	Alex
(and so on)		

RUSHING

The significance of 'thinking time' has been stressed elsewhere in this book. The downside of this is when teachers rush. The causes of rushing are usually inexperience, or insecurity about the behaviour of students. The latter means that the teacher is reluctant to leave a silence which can be filled by off-task talk or behaviour. The temptation is understandable: the cure is to establish (over time, perhaps) the ground-rules for question-based learning.

MANNERISMS

Mannerisms plague us all: but some mannerisms are more distracting for students than others. In questioning, mannerisms which have negative effects are often verbal; and they need to be eliminated as far as possible. As an example, I once had to supervise an initial teacher trainee who was a retired officer from the Royal Air Force. He was an engaging man, had a good rapport with the students, a firm grasp of his subject, and was an able classroom teacher. But he often responded to a student's answer with the single syllable 'OK' – he pronounced it 'oak'. Students being the delightful creatures that they are, soon picked up on this and began to exploit it: count the oaks in a lesson, how many oaks make a wood? . . .

Once aware of his behaviour, the teacher was able to eliminate this distracting mannerism entirely.

The commonest mannerism in question-based lessons is for the teacher to repeat the students' answers:

T: What is the capital of Peru?
P: Lima.
T: Lima – yes. How did you find that out?
P: I looked at the map.
T: You looked at the map. Exactly . . .

This little exchange is a caricature – but only just! When I raise this topic with teachers they often say to me: 'But other students don't always hear the answers given by a fellow student.' I accept that may be the case, but the solution is rather to encourage all students to speak up so that genuine classroom dialogue can take place. We need to return to the issue of establishing appropriate ground-rules.

A second mannerism that is all too common is that of the teacher repeating their own questions. This is usually to fill in the time between asking the question and obtaining a student response. Yet we have argued in this book that this gap is called 'thinking time' and should be used for that purpose. Repetition is legitimate if it is to clarify a complicated question, or to produce emphasis. Constant repetition is not a welcome mannerism.

Worst of all, perhaps, are the teachers who turn every question into a rhetorical or pseudo-question by simply providing the answer to it. These teachers have missed the point of questioning in the classroom; the apparent form of an open-ended lesson covers a didactic approach in which students are not treated as participant learners.

Mannerisms are hard to eliminate, mainly because we are unaware of them. Activity 32 suggests an unthreatening way of reviewing your mannerisms from time to time.

Activity 32

Eliminating mannerisms

From time to time tape-record a lesson or part of a lesson in which questioning plays a major role. In the privacy of your own home listen to the tape.

Listen for any irritating mannerisms which may distract the students' attention from your questions. Take appropriate action to eliminate them by becoming more aware of your classroom behaviour.

After a couple of weeks have passed do a re-test to see how successful you have been.

CHORUS ANSWERING

This is something which has to be addressed in a book of this kind; and it is one of the more controversial issues.

My own view is that there is little value in questioning for chorus answering. This view is supported by Cliff Turney (1975, Sydney Microskills Series 2: University of Sydney).

For me, there are two concerns about chorus answering:

1 Why am I asking this question in this way?
2 What do I hope to learn from the answer?

I feel that only the most trivial kinds of questions, or at least the lower order ones, lend themselves to this approach. Key Stage 2 teachers often use this method for things like mental arithmetic: Five 5s? Ten 7s? They justify it on the grounds of revision, reinforcement or practice. But 'bulk answers' to questions like this fail to reveal adequately what individuals in the class can do: i.e. they are poor questions even for feedback to the teacher, let alone encouraging students to think. Sharp children simply learn to delay answering for that fraction of a second until the best ones have! Then they mouth the answer quickly as if they knew it. They don't always deceive the teacher, but surely there must be a better and more discriminating way?

That's the case for the prosecution. James Dillon, however, tries to defend chorus answering. In the process he redefines the term slightly. He draws a parallel with Socratic dialogue in which the master leads a student towards an answer by gradually eliminating other possibilities. But this kind of dialogue is rather stilted for today's classrooms. He notes that in recitation questioning, as he calls it, the teacher speaks every other turn even if several students are involved. The students can only speak in (predetermined) answers, they can't engage in a dialogue. When they do speak they speak briefly. Answers tend to be only correct or incorrect. This is an example:

T: What is this here?
P1: The owl's foot.
T: Correct. And what do you notice about it?
P2: It's covered in hair.
T: Right. Now what would a foot be covered in hair for?
P3: To keep it warm.
T: No. Who has another idea?

Even Dillon, then, points out the rather limiting nature of chorus answering and recitation questions. But he does have an interesting sideline on the matter. He suggests that this method can be used productively, but with the students having time to prepare the questions about a piece of material they have had to investigate. The students then take the lead, and ask the questions of the teacher! This is an interesting concept, and one worth trying.

Outcomes

At the end of this chapter you should have:

- Examined each of the factors that might inhibit your skill as a questioner
- Practised distributing questions around the class more effectively to draw in non-participants and to control attention-seeking by some pupils
- Ensured that you are aware of, and take action about, any mannerisms you may have developed
- Become aware that these processes need to be repeated at intervals to avoid the development of poor habits in questioning.

14

QUESTIONING – WHAT THE RESEARCHERS SAY

OBJECTIVES

This chapter invites you:

- To take a tour through some of the insights into questioning and question techniques provided by researchers
- To compare and contrast your views and experiences with theirs
- To consider the concept of 'thinking time'
- To adopt a research-based approach to your own questioning.

This chapter is not intended to be a systematic review of the literature of, or current research into, classroom questioning; such a review is more appropriate in a research report. Rather the intention is to cull out some pithy sayings from those who have studied this subject area, and to use these as pegs on which to build thinking about questioning as a classroom skill. Connection is also made, as elsewhere in this book, with the current government documents listed in the Key References on page xi of this volume. This helps to point up that phenomena such as national standards do not materialise out of nowhere. While their history may not be acknowledged specifically, they are formed out of all or part of the professional wisdom of the time.

Finding material of this sort is not as easy as it might seem. Three of the most recent texts on pedagogy and pedagogical research do not even feature the word 'questioning' in the index (see reference 35 at the end of the chapter).

On the other hand, through using this manual, you are already on the road towards formulating your personal attitudes to, and skills in, questioning. So this chapter asks you to reflect on and refine your current views about the use of questions in the learning and teaching process. The quotations, with some brief commentary, are presented thematically.

A RATIONALE FOR QUESTIONING

1 *For over a century educators have emphasized the role of questioning in facilitating student learning. Yet our basic understanding of how questions might influence learning remains sketchy. (Thomas Andre)*

2 *There is no mystery to the use of good questions while teaching. (James Dillon)*

The first two quotations here stand in stark contrast the one with the other! This manual has tried to start to throw light on the issues implied in the first quotation. The Draft Handbook (TTA 2001) para 3.1.3 talks about 'key questions' as being part of clearly structured lessons, which themselves are aimed at producing improved attainment in pupils. You might find it useful at this point to review your own 'philosophy of questioning' using Activity 33.

Activity 33

Reviewing your rationale for asking questions
What do you think you have learned so far about:

- the importance of using questioning as a teaching/learning strategy?
- the purpose of questions as part of your personal philosophy of education?

Quotations 3–6 deal with raising the cognitive stakes in lessons. In this context, Rogers' quotation is an ideal, but Wragg's statistic (quotation 4) is salutary! On the other hand, one might take the more cynical, even sinister, view adopted by Barnes. Cunningham's view bridges the divide between the Rogers' ideal and classroom practice. The Draft Handbook places considerable, if often oblique, emphasis on improving cognition. It emphasises, for example, the use of assessment to measure progress (para 3.3.1). The aim of this process is to get pupils to 'think for themselves' (para 3.2.7).

> 3 *When problems of the future can no longer be anticipated and mass persuasion techniques exert a greater influence on the public than ever before, people must be able to think towards responsible choices and decisions. Educators must develop skills for evaluating cognitive levels of thought and methods of raising the cognitive levels at which children function. (V.M. Rogers)*
>
> 4 *57% of primary teachers' questions were related to class management. (Ted Wragg)*
>
> 5 *One interesting facet of the classroom relates to the ways in which the teacher covertly signals to his pupils what their role as learners is to be. (Douglas Barnes)*
>
> 6 *Questioning is one of the best ways for you to express humanistic attitudes involving respect for (students') ideas, freedom of choice, self-expression and honesty ... Most suggested approaches to teaching today encourage the teacher to act as a guide to learning. One does this primarily through questioning. (Roger Cunningham)*

In the quotations which follow we move on to look in more detail at the process of asking effective questions, i.e. questions that ask students to think deeply and productively. This kind of process fulfils the Draft Handbook's aspirations that teachers should be able to 'encourage pupils to reflect on and explain their thinking and reasoning' (para 3.2.1). The reservation of quotations 8 and 9 may underpin para 3.2.1's requirement to 'use and teach precise vocabulary appropriate to the subject, to help pupils be more articulate and conceptualise thinking strategies'. Later in the same paragraph, the Draft Handbook – like quotation 11 – requires the teacher to 'recognise and acknowledge success in pupils' thinking'.

> 7 *[As questioner] ... the teacher will play a more provocative role in raising issues and discussing ideas ... The questions posed need to be open-ended and designed to move forward the pupils' thinking. Alternative points of view should be generated, encouraged, tolerated. (The Arts in School Project Team)*

> 8 *By requiring short, factual answers, teachers may actually inhibit pupils' intellectual activity. (Neil Mercer in Bourne)*

> 9 *[Pupils] need to please the teacher by attempting to offer the answer that they think the teacher wants ... (Maurice Galton)*

> 10 *Current intelligence-testing practices require examinees to answer but not to pose questions. In requiring only the answering of questions, these tests are missing a vital half of intelligence – the asking of questions. (Robert J. Sternberg)*

> 11 *What comes through again and again from Galton's work is the importance of high levels of questioning and the need to engage strategies which allow maximum levels of sustained interaction with all pupils ... this would be consistent with Vygotsky's theory. (Caroline Gipps)*

The final block of quotations in this section of the chapter collects together some thoughts about process and its effects. In quotation 12, attention is drawn to the fact that teachers may develop bad habits in questioning, as well as good ones – hence the need for self-analysis, as recommended throughout this manual. Quotation 13 reminds us that our students' perceptions of us may be rather different from our own: our behaviour may have to be explained before it can become meaningful and productive. The final quotation reminds us that the use of questioning is just one of a battery of skills and must be handled like other teaching and learning strategies.

> 12 *The numbers and types of questions asked by any given teacher tended to be similar across observed lessons, suggesting that teachers develop a style of question performance. (Trevor Kerry)*

> 13 *A five-year-old girl returned from her first day at school and announced that her teacher was no good because she didn't know anything. When asked why she thought that, she replied that her teacher 'just kept asking us things' ... (George Brown and Ted Wragg)*

> 14 *Teaching comprehends more than one classroom action; it involves forethought and afterthought as well. The activity that constitutes teaching begins in an act of planning and design, continues in classroom action, and ends in a reflective act of evaluation and redesign ... The teacher's use of questioning follows a similar course. (James Dillon)*

QUESTIONS, LANGUAGE AND CLASSROOM LEARNING

The views of teachers about questioning, and those of researchers, do not always coincide. This is well illustrated in quotation 15 (a quote from an anonymous teacher in the researchers' project) compared with quotation 16 (the view of a researcher who studied the field in an almost unique depth but whose approach is more theoretical and analytical). The first of the two represents something akin to a chaos theory of questioning, while Dillon has a structure that removes most, if not all, of the ambiguity from the process of classroom questioning technique.

> 15 *I consider it almost impossible to define questioning. The techniques change with the mood of the teachers and the class. The ability level, the subject, the personality of the child, the time of day, where the lesson is being held etc., influence the questions we ask. (George Brown and Rowena Edmondson)*

> 16 *This scheme for teacher questions empowers us to take action by preparing, posing and pondering questions. The action consists of our ... answers to seven generic questions [i.e. about our own use of classroom questions]:*
>
> 1. *What are the questions for?*
> 2. *How to prepare them?*
> 3. *How to pose the question?*
> 4. *Who is to answer?*
> 5. *What to do with the answer?*
> 6. *How did the questions work?*
> 7. *Which next questions will work better?*
>
> *(James Dillon, p. 63)*

The next few quotations examine more or less explicitly the context of questioning. Both Barnes and Bridges see questioning as taking place in the context of classroom discussion. The Draft Handbook para 3.2.1 reflects that view, demanding that teachers 'use interactive teaching strategies and collaborative group work to encourage and challenge pupils to think and discuss'. For some, this may seem too vague or open-ended, since discussion implies to many an informal approach to teaching redolent of discovery learning, and typifying subject areas where right answers may be less relevant. The Draft Handbook goes on to analyse this process into factors such as: making inferences, detecting contradictions, ordering and sequencing, examining consequences and making judgements (para cit.). This is an issue too extensive to be discussed here, but you might like to look at Chapter 16 for a brief review of questioning in the context of classroom discussion.

> 17 *A study of closed and open questions would throw light on the problem of dealing with private misconceptions, and upon the value of discussion. What is the value of encouraging pupils to 'think aloud' at length? What importance should be given to insisting that pupils make explicit what they have learned either outside school, or in non-verbal terms inside school? (Douglas Barnes)*

> 18 *I suggest that group discussion provides one of the most creative and educative contexts for questioning in the classroom, and that its nature and purposes might therefore usefully be explored by anyone concerned with questioning. (David Bridges)*

The next two quotations raise the reader's awareness of the complex area of 'thinking time', which topic has been discussed on pages 90 above. This is an area in which it is hard to give precise guidance, and teachers have to make fine judgements. The Draft Handbook promotes the 'pace' of lessons as important in their success (para 3.2.5), but is silent on the subject of 'thinking time' – unless one includes the process of reflection which is recommended as a teaching strategy. Perhaps the real key to understanding the balance between pace and thinking time is experience and practice.

> 19 *Part of the teacher's skill is to match amounts of time for responding, to the complexity of each individual question. (Trevor Kerry)*

> 20 *It is a strange fact of classroom life that pupils are habitually given less than a second to come up with an answer, and are habituated into encapsulating their answers into short staccato bursts ... If you prefer, you may listen for the answer that is forthcoming and for all of it that will come. In that way you may hear an answer that otherwise would remain unheard ... (James Dillon, p. 102)*

Activity 34

Assessing thinking time

For this exercise you will need to tape-record a lesson, or part of a lesson, in which you are using questions to explore a new topic. You will also need a stop-watch.

Record the lesson, and play it back later. As you play it over record in writing each of your questions. Then use the stop-watch to decide how long you waited for the students to answer.

Note also any relevant information such as whether you filled silences unnecessarily, prompted too soon, interrupted, or whether you waited both long enough to allow thinking time and long enough for the respondent to develop his or her argument or thought.

What lessons have you learned from this exercise. What might you do differently in future?

In quotations 21 and 22 there is an emphasis on the quality of responses from students; and this is an important area to ponder. Perhaps your findings under Activity 34 will already have allowed you to make some assessment of the quality of your students' responses.

> 21 *I believe also that the movement in words from what might describe a particular event to a generalization that might explain that event is a journey that each [student] must be capable of taking for [himself/herself] – and that it is by taking it in speech that we learn to take it in thought. (James Britton)*

> 22 *It is not easy to measure pupil participation, especially since it is the quality of participation that matters rather than its vociferousness. (Douglas Barnes)*

Unfortunately, the quality aspect of classroom answers is not always the predominant one, as Beynon in quotation 23 warns. However, Brown and Edmondson are a little more optimistic as a result of their research project, which used teachers' own responses to illuminate practice. The Draft Handbook (para 3.2.6) describes this process thus: '[teachers should] monitor individual responses in the course of teaching and create opportunities for less confident pupils to participate ... value responses and respond to misconceptions as they arise in ways that help pupils understand and self-correct'.

> 23 *It is evident that the question and answer pattern predominates [in classrooms] ... and that teacher questions are a confirmation of power relations ... teachers orchestrate 'right answers' by constantly providing indicators of what they define as valid ... (John Beynon)*

> 24 *The most common reasons [for asking classroom questions] were encouraging thought, checking understanding, gaining attention, revision, and management. (George Brown and Rowena Edmonson)*

In addition to the quality of responses, we need to sustain the quality of our classroom questions. This is succinctly put by Brown and Wragg's first observation, below. Their second remark explains something of the tactics that teachers in their research project adopted in formulating questions and moving towards student learning.

> 25 *Questions are only as good as the answers they get. (George Brown and Ted Wragg)*

> 26 *Transcripts of lessons from the Leverhulme Project in which questions were thought to be used effectively suggest that teachers*

> *have in mind key questions around which are clustered a large number of briefer, more direct and specific questions. The lessons develop a pattern which may not always take a straight line, but is certainly not random. (George Brown and Ted Wragg)*

Our final quotation in this section reminds us that there is a direct relationship between the quality of learning and the quality of teaching. This insight was included in the Hay McBer report. It talked (para 1.3.8) about 'thinking teachers', and concluded:

> *The thinking that effective teachers bring to the job is characterised by Analytical Thinking – the drive to ask why, to see cause and effect and think ahead to implications; and Conceptual Thinking – the ability to see patterns in behaviour and situations and, at the level of outstanding teaching, to adapt creatively and apply concepts, ideas and best practice.*

This is high-sounding rhetoric, but what does it mean in practice? Hay McBer saw analytical teachers as those who 'show pupils the importance of a logical approach and get them to question why they are doing what they do on a regular basis'. Galton's Oracle Project research highlighted aspects of teacher style which produced effective learning. Among these, the ability to ask effective questions, and cognitively demanding ones, was also a factor.

> 27 *Galton ... classified ... teachers into types and investigated pupils' progress in relation to these types ... Two groups of teachers were more successful ... The first group were those who were able to sustain high levels of questioning ... The second group ... had the highest level of challenging questions ... (Gipps in Bourne)*

PROVOCATIVE THOUGHTS FOR QUESTIONERS

This final section tries to indicate some of the problems relating to learning to question effectively. These include the difficulty of the process (quotations 28 and 29); the need to learn new skills (quotations 30, 31 and 32); and the failures of initial or in-service training always to provide adequate support (quotations 33 and 34).

> 28 *In attempting to help children reach for high levels of thought, many teachers experience considerable frustration and even exasperation because pupil responses remain at a low and unsophisticated level. (Cliff Turney)*

> 29 *A problem of matching arises with questions. Generating questions, the demands of which match children's differing abilities, is virtually impossible. (PRINDEP Report)*

> 30 *Silence is very odd teacher behaviour to which everyone in the room will have to accustom themselves, and which you the teacher will just have to learn in the first place. (James Dillon)*

31 *Sequencing questions is a subtle art. (George Brown and Ted Wragg, p. 22)*

32 *It is helpful, then, to think of questions not as isolated events so much as sequences which build up from small beginnings into endings which have cognitive significance. (Trevor Kerry)*

33 *In many teacher training courses there is still too little attention paid to such important basic classroom skills as questioning ... (Ted Wragg)*

34 *Process innovation [such as learning to question] is dependent on a motivated teacher developing the analytical skills and pattern of reflection and support appropriate to his or her own needs, and it is most successfully achieved through experiential learning. (Eileen Francis, QE p. 39)*

The quotations in this chapter are a selection of those which have either most influenced me, or – in some cases – most provoked me to disagreement. Collecting quotations around a theme is a useful way of understanding the debate about that issue, and also for raising your own awareness and self-awareness as a practitioner. For this reason you might find Activity 35 helpful.

Activity 35

Compiling your own collection of quotes on questioning

Start your own collection of quotes on questioning.

Use a small notebook or include them in your questioning file.

Each time you find an insightful or provocative quotation, make a note of it, along with its source and any comments of your own.

Outcomes

At the end of this chapter you should have:

- Gained an insight into questioning through the work of some key researchers in the field
- Practised your skills in giving pupils 'thinking time' to answer demanding questions
- Started a collection of research-based insights of your own into the skill of questioning.

REFERENCES FOR THE QUOTATIONS

1 Andre, Thomas (1987) 'Questions and learning from reading' *Questioning Exchange* 1.1, p. 47. (*Questioning Exchange* was a journal that had a following of English and American academics; in 1987 it changed its format.Volume 1.1

was a relaunch in new format, a seminal volume which collected the wisdom on questioning from around the world. Unfortunately the journal did not survive the worsening economic times. Many of the quotations in Chapter 14 come from this influential international summary.)

2 Dillon, James T. (1988) *Questioning and teaching: a manual of practice*, p. 5. London: Croom Helm. (Dillon was the driving force behind the *Questioning Exchange* journal; he has since written successful texts about questioning. Though this text has a 1988 date, it has been reissued until very recently.)

3 Rogers V.M. (1972) 'Modifying questioning strategies for teachers' *Journal of Teacher Education* 23.1.

4 Wragg, E.C. (1993) *An introduction to classroom observation*, p. 8. London: Routledge. (Ted Wragg is perhaps better known for his commentaries on contemporary education in the *Times Educational Supplement*. Teaching skills have been a continuing interest of his over many years; and all his early work was in interaction analysis.)

5 Barnes, Douglas (1969) *Language, the learner and the school*. Harmondsworth: Penguin. (Now a classic text, the ideas in it have been very influential in all subsequent work on classroom language.)

6 Cunningham, Roger (1977) quoted from Weigand, J. (1977) *Implementing teacher competencies*. London: Prentice Hall.

7 Arts in School Project Team (1994) 'Teaching the arts' in Bourne, J. (1994) *Thinking through primary practice*, p. 146. London: Routledge.

8 Mercer, Neil (1994) 'Language in educational practice' in Bourne (*op. cit.*) p. 91.

9 Galton, Maurice (1994) 'Negotiating learning, negotiating control' in Bourne (*op. cit.*) p. 53.

10 Sternberg, Robert J. (1987) in *Questioning Exchange* 1.1, p. 11.

11 Gipps, Caroline (1994) 'What we know about effective primary teaching' in Bourne (*op. cit.*) p. 30.

12 Kerry, Trevor (1987) 'Classroom questions in England' in *Questioning Exchange* 1.1 p. 33.

13 Brown, G. and Wragg, E.C. (1993) *Questioning* , p. 33. London: Routledge. (George Brown has studied classroom language in both school and higher education settings; this book was produced as part of the Leverhulme Project into primary education.)

14 Dillon, James (1988) (*op. cit.*).

15 Brown, G. and Edmondson, R. (1984) 'Asking questions' in Wragg, E.C. (1984) *Classroom teaching skills*, p. 99. London: Routledge. (This work was reported as part of the Teacher Education Project in the universities of Nottingham, Exeter and Leicester – a secondary-based project designed to improve initial and in-service teacher education.)

16 Dillon, James (1988) (*op. cit.*) p. 63.

17 Barnes, Douglas (1969) (*op. cit.*).

18 Bridges, David (1987) 'Discussion and questioning' in *Questioning Exchange* 1.1.

19 Kerry, Trevor (1983) *Effective questioning*, p. 33. Basingstoke: Macmillan. (Part of the Teacher Education Project materials – these materials remained in print until about 1994.)

20 Dillon, James (1988) (*op. cit.*) p. 102.

21 Britton, James in Barnes (1969) (*op. cit.*).

22 Barnes, Douglas (1969) (*op. cit.*).

23 Beynon, John (1987) 'An ethnography of questioning practices' in *Questioning Exchange* 1.1.

24 Brown, G. and Edmondson, R. (1984) in Wragg, E.C. (1984) (*op. cit.*) p. 101.

25 Brown, G. and Wragg, E.C. (19963) *Questioning*, p. 18. London: Routledge.

26 Brown, G. and Wragg, E.C. (1993) (*op. cit.*) p. 24.

27 Gipps, Caroline (1994) 'What we know about effective primary teaching' in Bourne (1994) (*op. cit.*) p. 30.
28 Turney, Cliff (1975) Sydney Micro Skills series 2. (Cliff Turney was part of an Australian team of teacher educators who produced materials from the University of Sydney which have been extremely influential in this field.)
29 PRINDEP (1990) *Teachers and children in PNP classrooms*, Evaluation Report 11. Leeds: University of Leeds.
30 Dillon, James (1988) (*op. cit.*) p. 165.
31 Brown, G. and Wragg, E.C. (1993) (*op. cit.*) p. 22.
32 Kerry, Trevor (1983) (*op. cit.*) p. 43.
33 Wragg, E.C. (1984) (*op. cit.*) p. 196.
34 Francis, Eileen (1987) 'Discussion development in Scotland' in *Questioning Exchange* 1.1.
35 The three texts referred to are:
Soler, J., Craft A. and Burgess, H. (eds) (2001) *Teacher Development: exploring our own practice*. London: PCP/Open University.
Zmuda, A. and Tomaino, M. (2001) *The Competent Classroom*. New York and London: NEA and Teachers' College Press.
Sugrue, C. and Day, C. (2002) *Developing Teachers and Teaching Practice: International Research Perspectives*. London: Routledge Falmer.

LEARNING FROM TRANSCRIPTS

15

OBJECTIVES

This chapter invites you:

- To reinforce what you have learned from the text by undertaking a multi-layered analysis of the transcript of a lesson.

In this chapter you will be asked to review what you have learned by working over a transcript of a lesson based on questioning. During the lesson the teacher will use a number of good techniques, and will also make some errors or omissions. There will be open and closed questions, and low order and higher order questions. Your task is to work over the transcript to extract from it as much analytical thought about the teacher's use of questions as you can.

The suggestion is that you undertake several kinds of analysis, reading through the transcript several times and concentrating on one aspect of question technique at a time. The teacher's questions are numbered in the left-hand margin. Activity 36 may help to guide your thinking.

Activity 36

Analysing a transcript

Undertake each of the following analyses – you can do this in any order, but the one suggested is the most logical.

1 Go through the transcript and score each question as either 'open' or 'closed'. Use a grid like this to record your findings.

Question	Closed	Open
Q.1	✓	
Q.2		✓

2 Now reread the transcript with a view to classifying questions as low or higher order. Use the grid (above), but extended as shown to record this additional information.

Question	Closed	Open	Low	High
			0,1,2	3,4,5,6
Q.1	✓		✓	
Q.2		✓		✓

To indicate which type of higher order question is involved use the modified version of Bloom (described on page 71) as indicated below:

3 Next make an assessment of the teacher's positive skills as a questioner. Do this by working over the transcript again and using such evidence as you can glean to answer the following questions about this extract of the lesson:

a) Did the teacher establish the ground-rules of procedure?
b) Did the teacher create an appropriate learning ethos?
c) Were the students curious about the topic?
d) Was investigation central to the learning process?
e) Did the students own their own problem(s)?
f) Were the students encouraged to take 'intuitive leaps'?
g) Were all contributions valued?
h) Was learning monitored by the teacher through questions?
i) Did the teacher 'raise the cognitive stakes'?

(If you need to refresh your memory about these skills, return to Chapter 9.)

4 Now revisit the transcript to try to establish what use was made of students' questions. Try to answer these questions, if the evidence allows:

a) Was time for student questions planned in?
b) Were student questions welcomed?
c) Were student questions used in a productive way?

(Chapter 12 contains some material which will help with your judgements here.)

5 Now try to assess whether the teacher made any obvious errors (refer to Chapter 13). These questions may help you:

a) Did the teacher repeat his/her own questions unnecessarily?
b) Did the teacher repeat student answers unnecessarily?
c) Did the teacher answer his/her own questions?

6 And finally . . . make an overall assessment of this teacher's use of questions. Imagine you are writing a short (150-word) report on this teacher's questioning skills – what would you say? The aim is to:

- point up strengths
- reveal weaknesses
- set one or two key targets for improvement.

Write your report now.

Transcript

1 T: Who can remember what we did last lesson?

Miles: We were learning about living creatures.

T: Yes, and today we're going to investigate another kind of living creature – but first you have to guess what kind of creature it is!

Paul: Has it got anything to do with the caterpillars we looked at last week, Miss?

T: I'm not going to tell you that just yet – in fact, I'm not going to tell you at all! But you may tell me ... later. First, I need to give you some clues about this creature here, in the box. I want you to get into groups of three.

[They shuffle rather slowly into groups, with some noise.]

2 T: Now, can we have some quiet? Some of you are not being very sensible ... That's better.

Joy: What do we have to do, Miss?

T: I'm going to tell you. I'm going to give each person in your

3 'three' a card. What do you notice about the cards?

Tony: They're different colours.

4 T: How many different colours?

Gail: Three.

T: When you get the card, don't turn it over until I say; and don't show your card to anyone else in your three.

[Gives out the cards.]

T: Right, look at the card you have. On it is a clue about the creature in the box. Don't discuss your clue, but think about

5 what creature it is. Who thinks they know? If you think you know write your guess down. [Some write.] OK, so now pass your card to the person on your right in your 'three' and receive a card from the person on your left.

6 Now, who thinks they know? [A few more hands go up.] If you do, write the guess down without telling anyone!

Joy: What happens if we still don't know?

T: Well, when we've all seen three clues we'll see if anyone got it right. But we have to get some people with the answer before I open the box: my friend in there is very sensitive, and he won't come out if you don't work out who he is!

Dan: What do we do now?

T: Now pass the cards once again, in your 'three', so that everyone reads the last clue. [They do.] Right, one last chance for a guess – you've got quite a lot of evidence now.

Right – now those who thought they knew after the first clue, will you put your hands up? [Four hands go up.]

7 Melanie, can you tell us?

Melanie: Is it a chameleon?

[A few giggles – teacher controls with a look.]

	T:	Let's remember – we don't interrupt people who answer.
8		No, Melanie – but why did you think that?
	Melanie:	Because it said its head swivelled.
	T:	That's a good answer – but it's not right; you need to use the other two clues.
	Peter:	Can I tell you, Miss?
	T:	OK, Peter.
	Peter:	Is it a bush baby?
9	T:	No. Why did you say that?
	Peter:	Well, it's got big eyes, and it's small enough to go in that box!
10	T:	Logical – but what about the ears?
	Julie:	I think I know.
11	T:	What, then?
	Julie:	An owl?
	T:	Well, let's see what the others think. Look at all three clues.
12		What has: a head that can point backwards? Eyes as round as saucers? One ear higher than the other? So why an owl?
	Julie:	Because it has all three of those things, I think.
13	T:	What aren't you sure about?
	Julie:	The ears – you can't see an owl's ears.
	T:	Well, we'll look in the box and check it out.

[She opens the box carefully, and slowly withdraws a Little Owl.]

	T:	Here is my friend. As you can see, he looks vicious but he's not alive! He was a road accident victim and he's been stuffed. Now what I want you to do over the next 20 minutes or so is to tell me as much as possible about this owl, just from what you can piece together from what you see. I want you to deduce the lifestyle of this owl: how it lives, where, what it feeds on.
14		Who can start me off? What about you, Mark?
	Mark:	It's got a sharp beak.
15	T:	Good, what else about the beak?
	Nicky:	It's hooked and pointy.
16	T:	So what might that tell you about the owl?
	Jake:	It eats other creatures.
17	T:	Probably – so have we any other evidence of this?
	Tracey:	It's got very sharp claws – they could be for killing.

[The students feel the claws and comment on them.]

18	T:	They could. Which would kill more effectively – the beak or the claws?
	Georgia:	The claws.
19	T:	Right, so what do we think a Little Owl might kill?
	Chris:	Mice and things.
	T:	Well, that answer will do for now. So here's a creature equipped with claws and beak for killing and ripping. So,

still using observation, what else about this creature suits it
20 for killing? We say: how is it adapted for killing? The proper word is adapted so let's try to use that. How else is it adapted?

Tony: It's got soft feathers.

21 T: It has. So how does that help it?

Pupils: [Can't offer a reply.]

22 T: Anyone? [No answers forthcoming.]
OK, let's go back a step. The owl is a killing machine. We
23 know it eats mice. How does it catch them? You try to tell us, Karen.

Karen: Does it fly down and grab them?

24 T: It does. So how can soft feathers help?

Alan: Oh, is it that it doesn't make a noise?

T: Good. When it flies down it doesn't make a noise – just here, look, are even some special feathers that break up the flow of air so that it can move silently. I've got a bigger wing here, from a tawny owl, and look – when I flap it up
25 and down, what do you hear? [Demonstrates.] Nothing – that's what you hear!

Ruth: Is that why its feet are hairy, too?

[Some pupils giggle.]

26 T: Now, why the giggles? Ruth has made a good suggestion.
27 [To the gigglers] Had you noticed the hairy feet? [No reply.]
28 Well, Ruth is right – so very well done! How do they work to adapt this owl to kill?

Pupils: [Several incorrect solutions offered, half-heartedly.]

T: Well, think about it sitting on a post. A mouse rustles underneath it. It turns its flexible head to look round and down – the feathers keep it silent. It can fly silently after it takes
29 off – so what has it got to do quietly? [Longish pause; teacher scratches her nails on a desk top.]

Karen: Oh, I see – they stop its claws rattling on the hard post!

T: To stop them rattling, Karen – exactly that. So sum up
30 for us, Simon – how is this owl adapted into a killing machine?

Simon: It's got a moveable head ... it's got silent feet ... a hooked beak ...

T: Help him, someone ...

Paula: ... sharp claws for ripping it up into little tasty bits!

Wayne: ... special wing feathers ...

T: Good, you've got the idea ... And something else we still haven't discussed – those ears set at different levels on its head. Now you will have to take my word for it, but if we took all the feathers off this owl's head we'd see two big holes in the skull – the ears. One is higher than the other and this allows it to use the sound like a sort of radar, to pinpoint the direction very accurately: like this. [Draws a diagram on the board.]

Tina: But how can it eat something like a mouse – it can't cut up all the bones and that – why doesn't it choke?

T: That's a good point. We used a word just now, a technical word, that meant that the creature had some special features

31 – what was the word?

Jake: Adapted.

T: Yes. And this owl's insides are adapted so that it can swallow and digest prey like mice. Now I'm going to show you how that works later, maybe next lesson, but first I want you to draw some conclusions about this owl's lifestyle. You make some suggestions and I'll jot them on the board ... [She writes.]

Daren: Lives in fields.

Karen: Hunts small animals.

Ruth: Sits on posts – watching.

Simon: Moves silently.

Paula: Rips up its prey.

Angela: Hunts at night.

T: Yes, that's the big eyes, which we haven't talked about ...

James: Can owls really see in the dark, Miss?

T: Yes and no – they can't see if there is absolutely *no* light at all, but think about us. Imagine you are in a big barn at

32 night with just one candle to light it. Could you see anything?

Chris: Yes, a bit – some round the candle, and then dimmer as things got further from the light.

Ben: Are you scared of the dark, Miss?

T: Don't let's worry about that now – we're in a barn and even we can see something; the owl could see even in about

33 1,000th of that candle's light; and what else helps him?

Lisa: His radar ears.

T: Exactly, his radar ears – a good expression.

This lesson we have learned a new word – adapted. I want to tell you another new word. The owl lives in a field or a hedgerow, and it breeds there; so does anyone know

34 what this place is that the owl uses – what the technical word is?

Liz: Area.

T: No – but you've got the right sort of idea. The owl lives on

35 an area of land – what is the proper word for that area?

Bridie: Its home?

T: No ...

Jane: Its territory.

T: Well done, Jane – its territory. We'll use that word again next time.

Sadly, we are running out of time in this lesson; but we'll

have a look at how an owl's digestion works next lesson, and see if it eats caterpillars as someone hinted at the beginning of the lesson.

Between now and then I want you to think about a problem that you might have if you were an owl.

This is the problem:

To stay alive I need to eat three mice a day; and so does my mate. We have two young in a nest, and we need to catch two mice for each one, every day, for six weeks. How
36 many mice do my mate and I have to catch during the six weeks?

I've written the problem on a sheet which you can get
37 from Samantha as you go out – will you give them out for me, please, Samantha? – Line up quietly for lunch . . .

END-NOTE ON WRITTEN QUESTIONS

This book has examined the skill of classroom questioning by the teacher, along with related matters such as the role questions can play in helping students to articulate their learning. Our exclusive concern has been with oral questions. However, the same basic principles can be applied to written questions and their use in classrooms, too.

In this book there has been no attempt to extend into the field of written questions, because the matter is taken up and discussed at length in the companion volume *Learning Objectives, Task-setting and Differentiation,* to which you are referred.

A KEY TO THE ANALYSIS OF THE TRANSCRIPT

The numbers 1–37 refer to the marginal numbers in the transcript text on pages 125–129.

1 Closed type 1 (revision)
2 Open (or pseudo-open – there should be no choice) type 0 (management)
3 Open type 2 (the answer is in front of them so it's comprehension)
4 Closed type 2 (it's closed because there is a limited range of answers)
5 Open type 0
6 Open type 0
7 Open type 0
8 Open type 4 (turns a wrong answer into an analysis question)
9 Open type 4
10 Open type 4 (may include both analysis and application of knowledge, 3)
11 Open type 0
12 Open types 4, 5, 6 (any or all could be implied)
13 Open type 0

14 Open type 0 (the 'target' is closed: Mark)
15 Open types 3, 4, 6
16 Open types 3, 4
17 Open type 4
18 Open type 6 (a judgement needed) but may involve thought processes of types 3, 4, 5 too
19 Open types 3, 4, 6
20 Open type 3
21 Open types 3, 4
22 Open type 0
23 Open type 4
24 Open types 3, 4, 6
25 Open type 2
26 Open or pseudo-open type 0 (she is actually managing the situation)
27 Closed type 0
28 Open type 4 (3)
29 Open type 3
30 Closed type 1 (because the pupils have been given the answer)
31 Closed (one correct answer) type 1 (they've just been told)
32 Open types 2, 6 (the key word here is 'imagine')
33 Pseudo-open but actually closed (restricted answer) types 3, 4
34 Closed (one correct answer) type 1 (answer given last lesson)
35 Closed type 1
36 Closed (one correct answer) types 3, 4, 5
37 Pseudo-open (no real choice) type 0

With respect to the teacher's skills, there are examples of all nine elements within the transcript. She reminds them not to interrupt others. The lesson keeps the children engaged. The student questions signal curiosity. The whole lesson was based on 'finding out', beginning from the riddle. She won't open the box until some at least have struggled to a correct answer. There are several examples of intuitive leaps, beginning from the clues. The teacher accepts and uses even incorrect contributions and protects Ruth when the others laugh at her. She checked their knowledge of technical terms several times. The lesson contains examples of moving from low order to higher order questions as indicated in the sequences documents above.

Outcomes

At the end of this chapter you should have:

- Practised the use of the skills of questioning outlined in this manual by analysing a transcript of a lesson from several different perspectives
- Understood that all the same principles of questioning apply to written, as well as spoken, questions.

Questioning and discussion

16

OBJECTIVES

This chapter invites you:

- To consider the interplay between questioning and class discussion as teaching techniques
- To be aware that there are different ways of conducting discussion in class.

This chapter is intended to be a short review only of the place of questioning within classroom discussion.

One of the problems we have in reviewing this topic is to define what a classroom discussion is. In the 1960s an eminent and very talented educator, Professor Laurence Stenhouse, developed a form of discussion through which youngsters could learn about what he labelled 'issues'. Issues in this context include any topic which is controversial: war, relations between the sexes, acceptable social behaviour, drug-taking, and so on.

Stenhouse believed that real education took place when the students made up their own minds on these issues. For this reason he developed the concept of the teacher not as guide and facilitator, but as neutral chairperson. He felt that the teacher should always stand outside the issue itself, helping the students to explore it and balancing any bias in their arguments – but always taking a neutral stance.

The balance was achieved through vast packages of resource materials. As a discussion developed the teacher fed in pieces of source material which balanced views that the students put forward or which introduced new evidence that might alter their thinking. Under the issue of war, for example, strongly expressed antipathy to Germans for bombing London was to be balanced by source materials about British raids over Dresden.

Stenhouse's approach was a laudable one. The teacher posed careful questions designed to provoke the students to explore evidence, sift its veracity, draw conclusions and ultimately to reach a considered view. The questions tended to be higher order questions because that was essentially the nature of the exercise. But the method itself was quite controversial, many teachers found neutrality hard to achieve (there are some interesting debates which could be had around this point alone!), and they needed to develop quite sophisticated questioning techniques. These factors, combined with Stenhouse's premature death, put an end to a widespread use of this method of working in schools. One could argue that there were, at the time, people in positions of educational and political power who were quite glad to see the back of this approach: thinking citizens can be pretty uncomfortable to live with!

But this should not blind us to the very real merits of what this issue-based approach had to offer. The questioning skills were critical in this system, and many teachers learned much from it. The philosophy of the approach, too, has a certain intellectual attraction.

Dillon's view of what a discussion is is not so very different from Stenhouse's in terms of the format of dialogue involved. He points out that what characterises discussion is that teachers pose the initial problem through a question. But then they stand back and do not talk at every other turn (contrast the idea of recitation discussed above in Chapter 13). Students may hold the floor with interactive dialogue between themselves for quite some time. Teachers may intervene with further questions to focus the course of the discussion if it loses its direction. Inevitably, the questions used tend to be open rather than closed – closed questions, by definition, bring discussion to a halt. Generally, questions will demand higher order thinking processes from students. The questions used in discussion do not have 'right answers'. Teachers may use questions quite sparsely – but they will be very telling in guiding the direction and quality of student thought.

There is a sense in which the argument of this part of the book has now come full circle. In Chapter 8 it was suggested that we need questioning skills to encourage quality learning, because learning takes place through classroom dialogue. In the chapters which have followed we have examined some individual aspects of those questioning skills. Now, at last, we have returned to consider the place that questions have in one specific form of classroom dialogue – a form which achieves two important intentions:

- to provoke quality learning in students, and
- to do so through the stimulus of open and higher order questions from the teacher.

All that remains for you, the reader, to do is to hone your skills and put them into practice in your own classroom.

Outcomes

At the end of this chapter you should have:

- Understood the role of questioning in generating class-based discussion
- Recognised that there are different kinds of discussion that may serve different learning purposes
- Opened your mind to allowing pupils to take initiatives in asking questions and seeking to widen debate.

---

17 Explaining, questioning, the teacher and support staff

Before concluding this text about classroom talk it is necessary to acknowledge that, while we have discussed the relative roles of teachers and students, another – and increasingly significant – group of educationists has been omitted. These are the support staff.

Even a year or two ago, while there were many such appointees in schools, their roles were relatively unsystematic, and their job descriptions varied from school to school. The roles were generally quite lowly, and they were little involved in the public profile of the school. Few were included in training day activities, and many were allowed to participate in only menial tasks. All that has changed.

Over the last two years, mainly as a response to what has been perceived as major overload of teachers with administrative chores, support staff have been appointed to ease teachers' burdens. But at the same time, the jobs carried out by such staff have been extended in scope and relevance to the core business of schools: learning.

The intentions of government in this regard have been made clear through such documents as the speech by Estelle Morris, Secretary of State for Education, to the Social Market Foundation in November 2001. The text of this speech set out the intention of the Government to employ substantially more support staff, and to hand them some roles traditionally the domain of teachers. Some of the suggestions – such as that of allowing support staff to supervise classes that had been set work by a teacher – were not well received by the profession. Nevertheless, the general trend outlined in the speech was welcomed; and subsequent documentation has taken the idea forward. Thus in the DfES document Education and Skills – a strategy to 2006, we read:

> ***Our targets are to employ at least ... 20,000 extra non-teaching staff and 1,000 trained bursars by 2006. (p. 17)***

In practice, the situation is more complicated than these few paragraphs would suggest. While schools employ people in roles that are readily understood, such as nursery nurse and special needs assistant or learning assistant, other roles proliferate. A research project published in 2001 (Kerry 2001) identified that there were many other different labels for the jobs that support staff did, and these included:

- ICT technical officers
- laboratory assistants
- non-teaching assistant
- ancillary
- welfare assistant
- child support assistant

- education care officer
- specialist teaching assistant

These titles did not include roles in which teaching/learning was not regarded as a primary concern such as:

- mid-day assistant
- receptionist
- school secretary
- administrative officer
- head's PA
- finance officer
- bursar
- school business manager

and so on.

Nor did these roles include the growing army of volunteers in schools, often but not exclusively parents. Neither did it include the one group who have a statutory duty for what happens in schools – the governors. The research explored the problems that revolved around these issues and came up with a number of important conclusions:

- Many of these personnel could be proven, by us or by other researchers, to be playing a significant role in the education of children.
- Sometimes these roles were direct, e.g. in the case of the parent listening to children read; and sometimes they were indirect, e.g. the finance officer facilitating good curriculum materials to be available as a result of careful management of resources.
- Few of the post-holders, and no volunteers, had job descriptions and those that there were proved less than satisfactory.
- The differences between the jobs carried out by paid employees and volunteers were often minimal.
- The proportion of support personnel to qualified teaching staff was growing, and was frequently 3:1 in favour of support staff in primary schools.
- Certain roles – such as that of ICT technical officer – were now integral to the success of the school (e.g. one school's ICT officers now earn several million pounds annually for the institution by translating teaching materials composed by qualified teachers into commercial products for other schools to use).
- Some 'support' personnel were either teachers or qualified professionals (such as educational psychologists), but behaved in a support role in classrooms and schools in which they might have a temporary or intermittent role.

These insights led us to a new conceptualisation of support staff in schools that went along these lines:

> *Support staff are all those people, paid or unpaid, who are not members of the regular qualified teaching staff and who are used by*

> *a school to support the learning of pupils. While they may not be involved (though they sometimes are) in the* teaching *of pupils, they are without exception involved either directly or indirectly in promoting* learning *by pupils.*

The Draft Handbook now recognises that reality. It says (para 3.4.9) that teachers should be able to:

> *Work collaboratively with specialist teachers and other colleagues and, with the help of an experienced teacher where necessary, manage the work of teaching assistants or other adults to enhance learning opportunities for all pupils.*

The Draft Handbook, rightly, points out that this competence involves the willingness and openness on the part of the teacher to be observed while teaching, but also to work collaboratively in achieving shared goals within the class (the whole of the text of para 3.4.9 is worth examining in detail).

Implicit within these skills, however, is the ability of teachers to be able to provide some professional development and help for the support personnel in promoting children's learning. It is recognised that, at present, there is no coherent system for initial and in-service training of such staff. While plans are in hand for this as this text is written, and ladders such as NVQ are coming on stream, national conditions of service and training are still some way off.

For this reason it has been thought important to look at the two key skills that make up this text – explaining and questioning – from a support perspective. While it could be argued that some teaching skills (planning or differentiation, perhaps) are the prerogative of qualified teachers alone, by the nature of their work anyone who supports learning must be able to explain and question effectively, on a one-to-one or small group basis at the least.

With this in mind, two proformas have been included in this chapter to help teachers observe and provide feedback on these core skills for their support personnel. By tackling Activity 37 you should be able to pass on some of your knowledge to others who share your goals of promoting learning in your classroom.

Activity 37

Training the support staff

If you have support staff working to you in your classes, think through the teaching/learning tasks with which they assist.

Decide, using the text of this manual to help you, what questioning and explaining skills they need.

Devise an appropriate training experience for them.

Negotiate the opportunity to deliver this training.

Proforma for observing explaining skills

Teacher: **Observer:** **Date:**

Class: **Time:**

Lesson/topic/theme:

Evidence of preparation/awareness of explanation type/audience needs:

Attention-capturing beginning:

Quality of sequencing (nothing omitted):

Suitability of language / definition of key terms, concepts:

Links with experience and use of examples:

Effectiveness of audiovisual aids:

Use of connectives, linguistic ploys, repetition:

Voice control; fluency; use of pace:

Ability to 'raise the cognitive stakes':

The feedback loop:

Evidence of student understanding:

Proforma for observing questioning skills

Teacher: **Observer:** **Date:**

Class: **Time:**

Lesson/topic/theme:

Evidence of preparation of key questions:

Use of appropriate language/content:

Distribution of questions:

Use of student responses:

Timing/pausing:

Prompting/giving clues:

Making progressive cognitive demands:

Encouraging student questions / using them productively:

Avoiding pitfalls (poor voice control, mannerisms, rushing):

REFERENCES

Kerry, T. (2001) *Working with Support Staff*. London: Pearson.
Morris, E. (2001) 'Professionalism and Trust – the future of teachers and teaching'. London speech to the Social Market Foundation, 29 November 2001.

List of activities

List of tables

List of figures and proformas

Index

WESTHILL ACADEMY
LIBRARY